THE CATECHISM OF THE CATHOLIC CHURCH:
Familystyle

We Believe

VOLUME 1

David M. Thomas, Ph.D.
& Mary Joyce Calnan

ThomasMore®
A DIVISION OF TABOR PUBLISHING
Allen, Texas

NIHIL OBSTAT
Reverend Edward L. Maginnis, S.J.
Censor Deputatus

IMPRIMATUR
Very Rev. Donald F. Dunn
Vicar General for the Diocese
    of Colorado Springs

October 5, 1994

The nihil obstat and imprimatur are official declarations that a book or pamphlet is free of doctrinal or moral error. No implication is contained therein that those have granted the nihil obstat and the imprimatur agree with the content, opinion, or statements expressed.

ACKNOWLEDGEMENTS

Scripture quotations are taken from or adapted from the Good News Bible text, Today's English Version. Copyright © American Bible Society 1966, 1971, 1976, 1993.

Excerpts from the English translation of the *Catechism of the Catholic Church for the United States of America,* copyright © 1994, United States Catholic Conference, Inc.—Liberia Editrice Vaticana.

DESIGN: Dennis Davidson

Send all inquiries to:
Thomas More Publishing
200 East Bethany Drive
Allen, Texas 75002–3804

Printed in the United States of America

ISBN 0–88347–295–3

2 3 4 5 6   00 99 98 97 96

Contents

It is the tradition of families to hand down their most treasured possessions from one generation to the next. Each new generation accepts the special gift with great reverence, because it connects the family with its history, identity, values, and stories.

It is in this tradition that the family which is the Church has treasured the gift of faith and the inheritance that the Creator bestows on us as the children of God. The gift of faith has been treasured and preserved down through the ages in the stories of Scripture, the teachings of the Church, the writings of saints and scholars, the celebrations of sacramental life, and the witness of lives of love and service.

In this spirit, our Holy Father Pope John Paul II convoked an extraordinary assembly of the Synod of Bishops in 1985 which began the task of drafting a compendium of Catholic doctrine to insure that the inheritance of our faith story, values, and traditions would be accessible to and suited for the generations of the present and the future. The *Catechism of the Catholic Church* is primarily a resource of doctrinal, moral, social, and spiritual teaching for all those who have been given the responsibility of passing on our faith inheritance.

David Thomas and Mary Joyce Calnan have taken the *Catechism* down from the shelf, as it were, have given it life, and have made it an inheritance that will be passed down from family to family, from generation to generation. Their four-volume *Catechism of the Catholic Church: Familystyle* is the first local or national catechism written from the original resource. They are faithful and careful stewards of the Church's treasure of faith and values. First, they have divided their familystyle catechism into the same divisions as *Catechism of the Catholic Church*—Creed, Sacraments,

Life in Christ, and Prayer. Second, the reader can follow the development of topics in the same order as the new *Catechism*. Third, they connect the doctrine of our faith to the reality of life today in a process and style that touches your heart and your spirit. By adapting the *Catechism* to the culture and lifestyle of the family, they "unwrap" the *Catechism* and allow us to know our God as intimately caring and as connected to our everyday lives.

David and Mary Joyce are exemplary disciples of the Master Teacher as they skillfully and sensitively tell extraordinary stories of ordinary people, which draw you into the Word of God in Scripture and into the particular teaching of our faith tradition. Each chapter invites the reader to reflect on story, Scripture, doctrine and then to apply this to his or her own life as a family member. Each chapter concludes with a prayer for the rich resource of Church tradition adapted to the language and life of the family. Although this resource is intended primarily for families in all the many shapes and forms of family systems today, I believe that *The Catechism of the Catholic Church: Familystyle* will be a special gift to everyone in catechetical, liturgical, and other pastoral ministries as a resource and as a spiritual companion.

I am deeply honored to be invited to write the foreword for this book. David Thomas and Mary Joyce Calnan have a rich background in family life ministry. Their *Catechism of the Catholic Church: Familystyle* reflects that ministry as this work brings faith to life and life to faith. I know that readers will join with me in expressing my deepest gratitude for this gift of faith and love that will undoubtedly become a new classic in American Catholic spirituality.

Howard J. Hubbard
Bishop of Albany, NY

Introduction

Welcome

Before the front door of many homes lies a welcome mat. So in the spirit of a welcoming family, we say, "Welcome to your family book of faith." We have written this book for families. Thus, we do not use a language of theory or pure ideal, but one that you use daily in your conversations with your family.

In this family book of faith, we share some family stories, thoughts, feelings, and values about our shared Catholic faith. When we wrote this book, we had each and every Christian family in mind.

Recently the Roman Catholic Church published a comprehensive collection of the contents of the Catholic faith. The book, called *Catechism of the Catholic Church*, was the result of many years of conversation around the world. The Church wrote the cate-

> *The heart of faith blended with the heart of family.*

chism for Catholics everywhere, as a reference for bishops and other leadership, and for publishers.

A catechism is a collection of beliefs. The authors of this new catechism recommend that each country translate it into the language of its own people. In our familystyle catechism, we have done a double "translation." That is, we have adapted the catechism both to the language of our culture and to the language of the family. We have taken the heart of the faith and blended it with the heart of your family.

This familystyle catechism appears in four small volumes, which correspond to the four parts of the new universal *Catechism of the Catholic Church:* Creed (Beliefs), Sacraments (Celebrations), Life in Christ

(Morality), and Prayer (Spirituality). In this translation, we stress the ideas that are important for our families. In some places we added extra material, which is not in the larger catechism but which is important to the home. For example, we have provided expanded information on how families share faith, values, and their sacred, sometimes quite ordinary, moments.

As you begin this first volume of your family catechism, you will note its conversational style. As we wrote, we pictured ourselves sitting around the kitchen table with you just "talkin'." We believe that good family books are homey. Their covers often bear the imprint of chocolate-covered fingers. You can read good family books in kitchens, bedrooms, family rooms, and bathrooms. Because your family is probably short on time, the chapters of this book are short too.

> *Good family books often bear the imprint of chocolate-covered fingers.*

As you explore this book, you will discover that we use a broad understanding of family here. What do we believe about families? (1) Families are already holy in loving one another. (2) Families are systems. Because of this, whenever this book affects one individual, it also affects the whole family. And, (3) families are diverse.

We also believe that the word *family* has a different meaning for each of you and that the broader church needs to help families better appreciate their importance for both church and society. Finally, as you read this book, you will discover that we are convinced that in everyone's life there exists both a family dimension and a faith dimension. This family book connects the two.

Each chapter of our family book of faith has a specific theme. The book approaches this faith theme in four ways, which are based on the following statement about families: *"The family . . . listens . . . with faith . . . for the journey."*

"The family . . . ," which begins each chapter, is a brief story based on a family happening. The stories are fiction for the most part, although we based some on true experiences. These stories encourage you to walk around within a family environment as the chapter relates families to faith.

" . . . listens . . ." is our connection with the Bible. Your family listens to the Word of God at church, and you read and study the Bible at home. You listen to hear God's Word in your life because you know God is deeply interested in what happens in your family.

> *We searched the Scriptures and found treasures about families.*

For this book we searched the Scriptures and found some wonderful treasures that relate to each chapter's story about families and to the faith theme.

" . . . with faith . . . " brings to your attention the teachings of Catholic tradition. This part of each chapter follows the general topical outline of the *Catechism of the Catholic Church*. In this family catechism we help you reflect on these teachings and relate them to your family life.

" . . . for the journey" provides you with a focused reflection that stems from the family story in the chapter, the biblical passage, and your faith tradition. This section stimulates your thinking and invites you to apply the topic to your own family life.

Each chapter concludes with a prayer. Central to the faith and prayer life of the Church are the psalms, which are part of the Bible. The Church uses these psalms in the celebration of the sacraments. However, they also form the heart of what Catholic tradition calls the Liturgy of the Hours (the official daily prayer of the broader church). Vowed sisters or brothers in the religious life and priests or deacons say this prayer. Many lay people also say all or part of the Liturgy of the Hours each day.

Each chapter in this book ends with a psalm, or part of a psalm, that relates to the specific faith topic of the chapter. Following this psalm is an adaptation for your family. We wrote each adaptation in family language and used the details of your family's life in it. This prayer is for your home.

As the authors of this collection of small books, we want to share with you something about ourselves.

Where is God's grace in all this family stuff?

We wrote each of the four books of this family catechism from the standpoint of each of our unique life experiences. These experiences are the heart of our qualification to write this collection.

Both of us have spent years and years reading about, observing, and interacting with all kinds of families! Family has been our life work. All along the way, both of us independently asked a simple question: Where is God and where is God's grace in all this family stuff?

As colleagues in family ministry, the two of us discovered that while our curiosity and search had been the same, our journeys had been quite different. One of us was born in the mountains of Montana. The other, in the flatlands of northwest Indiana.

One of us learned a lot from the direct experience of family, raised three children, pieced together wisdom wherever it was found, and then received formal education including a master's degree in family ministry. The other learned from formal education (two master's degrees and a doctorate) and then entered the academic community as a professor, while raising a family with his wife.

A very important gift to this work is the fact that one of us is a woman and the other a man. Lots of differences all along the way!

We decided to join our differences and use our similar gifts to create for families. Everything we do, including this work, will answer the question, Where is God? The two of us agree: God is here among us! Right in the middle of our family!

While this belief was obvious to the two of us, it is not always so for everyone. Books on formal theology mention very little about family life. Spirituality books seem written primarily for the individual believer. We discovered that few authors had written about faith in ways that spoke to the experience of family and used the language of the family. In fact, we began to realize that few writers wrote about how ordinary family life is central to the life of the Catholic faith.

Thus this project was born. Here we create a catechism with your family in mind from start to finish. Your family must always attend to basics. So must your faith. In this book, we join the two.

And one final comment about what we, as the authors, bring to this faith book for families: We wrote this catechism in a Jesuit retreat house nestled in the foothills of the Rocky Mountains just outside Denver, close to where one of us lives with *God is right in the middle of family!* his family. We want to acknowledge the warm hospitality of the Jesuits and staff who are part of this holy place. Both of us believe that writing in a building dedicated to silence, reflection, and prayer operated by a religious community gives a deeper meaning to our work.

As people came in and out to pray and be touched by the grace given in this holy place, we recognize family people—those for whom we are writing. And although your home is usually the opposite of a place of silence, it is nonetheless holy; it is a place of reflection and prayer.

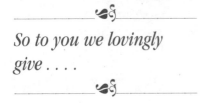

So to you we lovingly give . . . .

Your home is also operated by a religious community—your family. Writers often summarize Jesuit, or Ignatian, spirituality with the phrase "to find God in all things." We found God in both places—the Jesuit retreat house and our own homes.

Permit us to leave our welcome to you with a dedication of this work to our children. We do this because they are the ones entrusted to each of us and our families, by our God, to love and nurture in the faith and then, with love, to let go in faith.

So to you, Paul, Erin, and Michael,
and to you, Sarah, Michael, Peter, Joseph, and Timothy,
we lovingly give you this gift of our faith
in you and in your families.

Will they read this? Who knows. You know what family is like!

CHAPTER ONE
Our Hunger for God

"Oh, man, have I been waiting for this!"

The handsome eighteen-year-old sat by the front window with his new jacket. His thoughts ran in a jumble. "Let's see . . . did I forget anything? Wonder why they're late? Maybe I'll eat lunch. Naw. Better check my room again . . . Maybe I left something there. Geez, I'm really getting paranoid. Must be nerves. I wonder what it'll be like there. If all the hype about it is true."

"Wonder if Shep will miss me," he thought. "Gosh. I won't see him 'til Christmas, maybe not even then. He's a good dog! Hope Mom remembers his water."

He had so many feelings. Excitement, yes, and a creeping sadness, which he fought.

"Not that I don't like it here," he thought. "And I love mom and dad. But I'm ready for this. Oh, man, have I been waiting for this!" he exclaimed to himself.

"Hey, where is everybody? Think they'd hang around to say good-bye!" he said, as it dawned on him that he was alone.

"Hey, Mom! Dad! Are you downstairs?" he hollered.

As he rounded the corner of the storage room he found them . . . in a big hug . . . and crying.

"Oh, sorry . . . I couldn't figure out where you were. Um . . . m . . . m, I'm probably going to be leaving pretty quick," he stammered.

"We know," his dad responded, as they let go of each other and his mom turned slightly away to take care of her face.

"We were just coming up. Mom was down here looking for your first-day-of-school picture and found this," the father said.

The teen put his hand out to take the paper. It was obviously a little kid's picture on old construction paper. He saw a rather funny-looking tree, with a little person sitting at the top. Coming from the little figure's mouth out into the sky were the words "Someday I'll fly away!"

He looked up at the two people he loved most in all the world. No words came.

It was time to fly away.

"The desire for God

is written

in the human heart. . . ."

CCC, 27

The child grew and became strong; he was full of wisdom, and God's blessings were upon him. Every year the parents of Jesus went to Jerusalem for the Passover Festival. When Jesus was twelve years old, they went to the festival as usual. When the festival was over they started back home, but the boy Jesus stayed in Jerusalem. His parents did not know this. . . . On the third day they found him in the Temple, sitting with the Jewish teachers, listening to them and asking questions. All who heard him were amazed at his intelligent answers. His parents were astonished when they saw him, and his mother said to him, "Son, why have you done this to us? Your father and I have been terribly worried trying to find you." He answered them, "Why did you have to look for me? Didn't you know that I had to be in my Father's house?" But they did not understand his answer. So Jesus went back with them to Nazareth, where he was obedient to them. His mother treasured all these things in her heart. Jesus grew both in body and wisdom, gaining favor with God and people.

Luke 2:40–43, 46–52

Jesus decides to do something on his own.

The gospels tell us about Jesus' life. Yet they record only one story about his boyhood. It's the one printed above. What an interesting story! Jesus, on the threshold of being a teenager, decides to do a little thinking and acting for himself. Knowing that his parents are leaving for the long trip back home, he decides to stay behind and do something on his own. This is familiar to most families. We often experience a similar attempt on the part of our young. (In some families this begins at age two!)

While the biblical story seems rather simple, it contains important messages. To the Jewish people, the Temple was a sign of God's presence. It is there Jesus stays while his parents make their way north to their family home in Nazareth. He is not being rebellious; he is simply being faithful to his God.

What is the message here? That family is important, but our relationship to God is even more important. Even at the preadolescent age of twelve Jesus was teaching all of us. And he wasted little time in communicating to his mom and dad that God was first for him. He came from God and would return to God. So will we.

Note how Jesus relates to the adults in the Temple— the teaching staff. His questions impress them, and the more answers they give, the deeper his questions become.

When this one story from Jesus' childhood ends, Scripture tells us that Jesus was reunited with his parents and returned to his hometown of Nazareth for about the next eighteen years. We know next to nothing about what he did. We can assume, however, that he did something very important: He lived an ordinary life with his family! That in itself was and is holy.

> *". . . the person who seeks God discovers ways of coming to know him."*
>
> CCC, 31

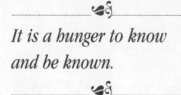

It is a hunger to know and be known.

The leave-taking described in the opening story is common in young lives. In fact, all through our lives we seem to look ahead. We await a time always coming, prepared for over and over. Before birth, before that very first cry, we were waiting. We are always seeking something; always needing someone.

And then after birth, this needing carries on through all our primary years. We need food, a warm bed, someone to hug us, someone to bandage our skinned knee. And later, we need money for jeans, or we long for someone to wait up when we are late again! Always we search and seek for the security of love.

The young man in our family story is searching too. His needs have grown up. In him is a hunger for life beyond the safe and comfortable life of his home. He has to go. His mom and dad know this. This leave-taking is not easy for any of them. But when the hunger of the body or the hunger of the soul becomes known, we must do something.

All of us can probably relate to his hunger. We know the body's hunger. But we know another hunger too—the hunger of the soul. This hunger is deep and powerful; it is a hunger to know and be known, to love and be love, to be—now and always.

We sometimes have so many hungers that we cannot count them. We hunger to know: Where did we come from? Where are we going? Is there a God? And when we come to believe there is, how do we relate to God? Does life have a meaning beyond death? Is there life beyond death? Really and truly? To satisfy the hunger of our mind, we seek answers from other people and from life itself.

We hunger for knowledge, yes. But we also hunger for love. We long to be loved and accepted for who we are. We want to love others deeply and honestly. We want to be connected to them.

We hunger, too, for life—for all of life. We want to be aware of what's inside us, beyond us, around us. We want to taste and feel all that life is and can be. This hunger for life is a deep desire to know that God loves us very especially. That we are dear to God.

In reflecting on this deep hunger within, we also know that this longing can disturb and confuse us, that it can create an anxiety within. Because this hunger may be uncomfortable, we often seek ways to quiet its presence.

Faith, however, helps us realize that this uneasiness serves as a powerful reminder that we are incomplete. We want more; we need more. And God made us this way. This is our belief: We were made for more. And what is that more? God.

The hunger is universal

Who am I? Is this all there is?

At this point in human history we are more aware of the thoughts and feelings and reality of people around the world than ever before. Media and other forms of communication connect us to one another. Thus, we have learned about the ways of human beings everywhere.

Because of this, we have also discovered that people everywhere search for answers about the meaning of love and of life. They may ask their questions in many different languages and ways, but they all search. And although people from all the corners of the earth formulate different answers, the questions are always the same! Together we ask: *Who am I? What is my life all about? Is this all there is?*

The questions are universal, a part of our human makeup, a natural part of us, built into our humanity. But are the answers natural too? And, an even more worrisome question: Are there any answers? Does God give us a hunger, fill us with questions, and refuse to fill our hunger, answer our questions?

Our faith says no; our faith assures us that we can find the answers to our deepest longings. God made us and put the questions within us. And God, who created the hunger in the first place, also provides the food, the answers.

At every age we experience this hunger

Earlier, we read the biblical story about Jesus and his boyhood experience at the Temple. He, too, was asking questions. Big questions stirred within him, just as they churn within us.

These hungers lead us forward.

Parents can relate to this, for what parent has not marveled at the depth of a child's questions at different stages along the journey? In fact, if we explore the searching from birth to death, we can see what God is doing, how the search is continual and real.

Because a family has members of various ages, we come to recognize typical questions over the life cycle. Knowing what to look for, we witness deep and developing human hunger all along the journey.

The infant in the crib calls out for food, for Mommy, for Daddy! The two-year-old child wanders from the yard, down the street, searching. "What's out there? Who's out there? Does God live in my neighborhood?" The five-year-old goes off to school to explore new places, find new friends, search out new ideas. The child asks, "Will I ever learn everything? Why do zebras have stripes? Is God bigger than our house?"

The preteen begins to hang out with the opposite sex. Questions explode within: Why? Am I okay? Is God different from me? Seeking independence, the adolescent shouts, "I want more; I like this! Can I really have it all? Is there a God at all? Do I need God?"

The newlyweds unpack their wedding presents in their new apartment. They carefully give a place to everything: the three toasters, the electric blanket, the special glasses that held the champagne at their reception in the church basement. They, too, wonder what lies ahead. How will they grow in the days ahead? (Their parents wonder too!)

Even older persons, in all their wisdom, still have questions. None of us ever knows "it" all! An older Jesuit priest once shared that he had learned just two things during his fifty years as a priest. He confided, "The first thing I've learned is that God is God, and the second is that I am *not* God. For all the rest I'm still searching!"

So God made us with this wonderful and disturbing hunger—a hunger that only one relationship will satisfy. This total relationship stirs us, invites us to discover the God, who is the other in this eternal relationship.

Along our journey, we learn that being a person with wants, desires, questions, and yearnings is okay. More than okay! It's the best way to be!

We who are *not* God were created by God. And this God gave us a hunger for more all along our journey. All along the way, God offers us all we need to know to make our journey happy and fulfilling.

But all along the way we find new hungers within us—hungers that keep us journeying. These hungers lead us forward, stay with us until we arrive at our destination. Then, we discover that the answer, the only answer to all our questions, is God.

**We're always going.
The Christian journey
is like that.**

As we grow, we spend a great deal of the time moving from one thing to the another: from first grade to second, from house to house, from one birthday to another, from friend to friend, from meal to meal, from day to day. We're always striving, seeking, changing, wanting, needing. But no matter how much we find, how much we achieve, we always want and need more.

The young man going away from home prepared himself for a trip. He packed his bags; he planned for his dog; he made plans for the future. As he did all this, he probably knew that at some point he would happily return home—for a while. Then he'd leave again. Jesus was probably glad to get home too. But he left again. He went and came back and went again. Trips are like that.

But our life journey is different. When we embark on that journey, we go forward and keep going. We never, ever, return. We're always going. The Christian journey is like that. We are always journeying toward the end of our life . . . and beyond.

On our Christian journey, we can take certain treasures with us: the vision of God that our parents or our family or our friends shared with us; our faith, the belief we have reached in our own search; our understanding of Catholic tradition, our daily leaps of faith when our children ask their innocent questions.

The treasures we pack for life's journey to God are varied and personal. We keep adding to them as we grow and change and find God in new ways through our family and through the daily events of our life. At the end of our journey, we discover what we have always sought: God's unconditional and irrevocable and inevitable love.

A Psalm

As a deer longs for a stream of cool water,
so I long for you, O God.
I thirst for you, the living God.
When can I go and worship in your presence?

Psalm 42:1–2

Family Hunger

As little children long for a hand to hold
And teens for a phone call,
So do we seek that which will fill us
   with joy
And lasting happiness.
You have made us for you, O God,
And we are given a clue of this
In that deep hunger
That will not go away.
Help us to accept our situation of need,
Our impatient desire for an eternal Christmas
When we will get all we want.
Open our eyes to see your beauty in spring flowers.
Help us feel your warmth in our family embraces.
Excite us for the journey each day.
Remind us that our love for each other
Is also our love for you.
Bless the holiness of our quest
And someday bring us all to a holy and eternal rest.
Amen.

CHAPTER TWO

God's Response to Our Need

Sitting on the porch by the flowing water . . .

She hated dealing with money! And trying to balance the checkbook and figure out if she had any left was the worst!

Now it was almost time for the baby to wake up, and she couldn't find the mistake! How was she going to afford any kind of party after the baptism, let alone some kind of outfit for the baby if she couldn't find out if there was any money!

"Oh, God. I hate doing this!" the young mother cried out loud.

Then she remembered the hose was still on. Probably flooding the basement! She flew out to the side of her small house.

All was well, so she stood for a moment and watched the water gently flow into the flower garden next to the porch. As the mailman approached the house, she greeted him and accepted a handful of envelopes.

"Thanks," she said, glad to see a friendly face.

Leafing through the pile of bills and junk mail she suddenly found one with familiar handwriting. A letter from her mother! Sitting on the porch by the gently flowing water, she opened the envelope and read:

Dear Kim,

Hello again, I am writing today to tell you to watch for a package coming soon. In it you will find the little outfit you wore when you were baptized. I was also baptized in it, as was Gramma.

Now, Kim, please know that I am not pressuring you to use it for your baby. I know you're trying to be independent and start your own life, and we're so proud of you.

However, perhaps you could just put it on him for a minute, to keep up the tradition. It really is so special, you know, having touched other precious newborns (like you!) in our family!

Also, since I can't be there to help, would it be okay if I sent a check to help pay for some of the celebration you said you'd be having after the baptism? This would make your dad and me feel that we were there in some small way. How our hearts ache to see him, and be there on that special day.

The young mother suddenly heard the water flowing from the hose again. She watched it as it gently soaked into God's warm earth.

Sacred Tradition and Sacred Scripture . . . are bound closely together . . . flowing out from the same divine well-spring . . . toward the same goal!

CCC, 80

Some people brought children to Jesus for him to place his hands on them and to pray for them, but the disciples scolded the people. Jesus said, "Let the children come to me and do not stop them, because the Kingdom of heaven belongs to such as these." He placed his hands on them and then went away.

Matthew 19:13–15

Someone in the crowd, perhaps a mom, noticed the children.

Jesus had a wonderful way about him! The ancient world mostly ignored children and women. Some societies simply counted them along with the farm animals and other household goods! However, Jesus, with his sensitive eyes, often searched a crowd to see whether anyone was being overlooked or not being counted.

And on this day, someone in the crowd, perhaps a mom, noticed the children and, against prevailing custom, brought them to Jesus. The disciples tried to block the entry of the children. They wanted to protect Jesus, to give him some time to himself.

But, like all of us, they still had some learning to do, and so Jesus responded to their misplaced concerns by scolding them. Strong words. In public too! Then Jesus gently drew the little ones to himself and touched them with love. For such is the kingdom, he went on to explain. God cares for all, even though we don't acknowledge or count some people as persons.

Let the little children come; I care, Jesus says. Both God's presence and God's response demonstrated by God here on earth! Like the young mother in our story, who cared and was concerned for her newborn, and like her mother, still caring and being concerned for her own now-grown child, God, too, cares.

In the sacred books,

the Father

who is in heaven

comes lovingly

to meet his children,

and talks with them.

CCC, 104

&

"You will be my
people."

&

In Chapter One, we reflected on the hunger within each of us for meaning. This hunger is great. We hear it in children and teens, in midlifers and older people. How terrible the tragedy if the hunger were never satisfied.

God knows our hunger; God knows we need more than just ourselves. And because of God's love for us, that more is both promised and given. The more is God's own self. We seek to fill our hunger; God seeks us out, offers us that which will complete us. God offers self.

In the scriptural story for this chapter, Jesus reaches out to the children. His care and concern for them is deep and real. He informs all those within earshot that the children are his and he is theirs. Once again, Jesus steps outside the boundaries of conventionality. He ignores his enemies who accuse him of being friends with tax collectors and known sinners, who were other unacceptable people at the time. He extends to all God's love. He invites all to accept God's fullness, a fullness that fills the hunger of each of us.

Jesus helps us understand that the human condition is one of need. God wants to fill that need by making us members of God's own family. The phrase, "You will be my people and I will be your God" summarizes this very important reality. But always, God respects our human nature. God does not force us into a relationship. Instead, God gently invites us, just as Jesus invited the children.

Family is about closeness and love—especially in hard times. Let's recall the story that begins this chapter. Kim and her mother belong to each other—they're family. The love and concern between them invites action. So the mom writes a love letter to her daughter. She communicates her love through the written word. How delighted Kim was to get this personal letter from a loved one.

In a way, family letters and cards are the sacred scripture of our families. Kim came to a deeper appreciation of her mom through the special love expressed in the writing (action) of that simple letter (word). God, too, shows love for us through actions and words, much of which is captured in the written word that we call the Scriptures, or the Bible.

Perhaps the best way to learn about others and about ourselves is through the telling of stories. We all love a good story! Good stories about others reveal us to ourselves. They help us make sense out of our own life as we search for meaning. The Bible is filled with stories. In fact, the Bible contains God's love stories. In these stories, God seeks us out, loves us, offers food for our hunger. Some of these stories are ancient. Still, they have the power to reveal us to ourselves!

Founding family stories of God

Scripture is filled with family stories.

Let's think about the story of Noah and his family. We can all relate to parts of this story—the storms and floods, the boats and animals, the fear of death, the possibility of hope, the happy ending. Sometimes people make light of Noah's story and poke fun at it. But his story is a serious one. It's about survival and about God's caring for both humans and animals. At the end of the Noah story, we see the rainbow, a truly wondrous sight symbolizing God's promise to be a God of life, not death.

And then later in the Scriptures, we learn about Abraham and his family. (Scripture is filled with family stories!) As this story goes, God invited Abraham to pull up stakes in the large (for those times) metropolitan area of Ur and head for the open spaces of the desert.

Next, God made a request of Abraham, a request that tested his trust of the God who had called him out of Ur. The biblical story says that God asked Abraham to do a seemingly terrible thing—to sacrifice his only son! Yet earlier in the story God had told Abraham that he was to be the father of a great nation and that his descendants would be as plentiful as specks of dust on earth. Truly, Abraham must have been confused. After all, having descendants is difficult if one has no children!

This request was a major test of Abraham's faith in God. Abraham was to accept that God knew what God was doing. Acting on his strong and abiding faith, Abraham was about to obey God's request when, at the last minute, God stopped him and provided a stand-in— a goat.

A good part of Scripture goes on to tell about the importance of all the descendants who came from Abraham, including Jesus himself. Abraham became known as a model of a faith-filled person. (Faith is always tested, and the choices are often hard.)

Scripture reveals God to us. And the fullest portrayal of God and God's love for us comes in the person of Jesus Christ, who is God with us, God living among us, God as one of us!

In the life of Jesus—in what he did and in what he said—we are given the fullness of revelation. That is, everything we need to know about God we can find in Jesus. When a person embodies a message or an idea, we meet wondrous mystery; a mystery that we can never fully understand, but also a mystery whose depths we can explore for all eternity. Of course, each of us is a mystery to others. But Jesus is the greatest and most important mystery because he is God with us.

The creation of the New Testament

They shared their stories about Jesus.

In the Church everything is directed at revealing God's love for us through the life, death, and resurrection of Jesus. God-become-human, Jesus, used simple words and simple actions; he taught with stories (usually family-related stories called parables). Their encounter with Jesus revealed to his listeners the depth of God's love for them. Everything he did and all that he was and is reveal the presence of God.

After Jesus died, those who walked the dusty roads with him, who remained close when he was crucified, and who encountered him after his resurrection from the dead became the primary storytellers or witnesses to the reality of God in Jesus.

These first witnesses, his followers, gathered interested people to tell them what they had seen and heard Jesus do and say. Then they talked about things Jesus had asked them to do to remember him. They shared their stories about Jesus, but they also remembered him through the breaking of the bread, the Eucharist. Soon, the apostles began to leave Jerusalem in order to communicate to others the wondrous story of Jesus. Eventually they moved to the far reaches of the world— at least as it was known to them.

Peter, a great friend of Jesus, traveled as far as Rome where he died by crucifixion as Jesus did. Thomas, another of Jesus' close friends, is said to have traveled all the way to India! In all these places the apostles shared their experiences and their stories, their memories. Listening to the apostles' stories, others found meaning for the hunger in their lives.

Gradually the original eyewitnesses began to die so the Christian believers decided to record the stories of Jesus in written form so that future generations could know them. The Church calls the four collections of stories the gospels.

Some early leaders also developed the tradition of writing to groups of new Christian communities that they had visited and to which they had preached Christ Jesus. These writings (of Peter, John, James, Jude, and Paul) eventually became part of what we now call the Second, or New, Testament. We call these writings letters, or epistles.

Of course, the pages of a fairly limited collection of writings could not contain everything Jesus said or did or was. Other things about Jesus became part of the lives of those early Christians. They formed a community of believers. The leaders of the Church preserved what they had received from Jesus. This became the tradition of the Church.

So today we have two sources that contain the revelation of God. One is Sacred Scriptures—the Bible. The other is the life of the Church, the gathered people, lived out as collected in our teachings. We call this second source Tradition. Each source complements the other, and we are still discovering the richness of God's revelation.

The preservation of God's revelation

The magisterium of the Church preserves the truthfulness and accuracy of God's revelation. However, the world is always

Part of the role of the Church is to update its teachings.

changing, and so are our culture and language. So part of the role of the Church is to update its teachings so that it can effectively communicate in different historical periods and to different cultures.

Thus the Church gathers its leaders from time to time in councils. At these meetings, the church leaders examine "the signs of the times" (a phrase used in Scripture) and relate them to the Church's teachings.

In a sense, this makes the Tradition of the Church a living tradition that is always open to a renewed awareness as times change. Thus, the Church remains faithful to the life and teachings of Jesus even in times of change.

The Second Vatican Council, which met between 1962 and 1965, was the last great council meeting held by the Church. Led by Pope John XXIII (who was known as the pope with a wonderfully open attitude), the meetings had a profound effect on the life of the Catholic Church. Most of the teachings of this catechism are connected with some important idea or teaching that comes from Vatican II.

For instance, the documents of Vatican II emphasize that those ordained to be leaders of the Church (pope, bishops, priests, and deacons) were servants to the rest of the Church. The one who was to be the greatest servant of all was the pope himself. So, the pope must remain faithful to Jesus' words and Jesus' example and must teach in a way that truly applies our tradition to our own time.

From time to time the exact formulation of the important beliefs of the Church may become cloudy or confused. The magisterium of the Church must preserve the accuracy of belief. The Church expresses these beliefs in precise language called dogmas. Sometimes the Church gathers the dogmas into longer forms called creeds. (A creed is a statement of what we believe.)

Most Catholics recognize the Apostles' Creed, which begins with the words "I believe," and the Nicene Creed, which begins with "We believe." Both creeds are brief and to the point; they summarize the Church's understanding of its beliefs at a certain point in history and they continue to address us today.

Through the life and teachings of Jesus, God offers us an understanding of the deep meaning of our life. Our faith response is an ongoing process, not a once-and-for-all event.

Let's hear God whisper to us.

We can all relate to a warm summer's day, a hose running, and anticipation of something like a child awakening or an upcoming family celebration such as a baptism. And, surely, the majority of us can relate to making our money stretch. Something we often ignore until it's too late!

And we can probably all relate to receiving a loving gesture that comes in the nick of time. Often we dismiss the event as an accident. However, as Christians we recognize the loving response of our God in these events that proclaim love.

Kim probably felt a great lump in her throat when her mother wrote about the little baptismal gown and its holiness to the family tradition. And she probably let the tears fall when she read about the money coming. And surely she felt a longing for her parents' presence at the baptism. All of this, done in love between two humans, reveals the love of God that Jesus proclaimed to us and showed us by his every action.

The story says that Kim watched the water "as it gently soaked into God's warm earth." Perhaps we might choose to look at the holiness of loving and caring for one another, as well as the quiet moments of watching water flow or gazing at a sleeping baby or listening to an elderly person remember the past. Wherever you look, you will recognize, in the midst of the ordinary moments of life, that which Jesus did and said and that which he invited us to be.

Let's enter our day today with our eyes and heart open. Let's hear God whisper to us. Quietly paying attention to God's world around us puts us more deeply in touch with the wonderful gift we have been given: life with one another and with our God.

A Psalm

O Lord, you have always been our home. / Before you
created the hills / or brought the world into being, /
you were eternally God, / and will be God forever. /
Fill us each morning with your constant love, / so that
we may sing and be glad all our life.

Psalm 90:1, 2, 14

When God Dwells in Family

Come be with us, O Lord Jesus,
On summer days and winter nights.
Open our hearts to listen to your word
When it hides in family words
Of love and challenge,
Of worry and hope.
Speak to us during family meals
(if you can edge in a word).
Talk to us as we sweep sidewalks and garages.
Keep the elevators moving as we rise to our home,
Or keep that back road open amid the blizzard
     on the farm.
Walk with us as we push shopping cart
     or wheelchair.
Within the quiet conversations before bedtime,
Let us know your care
For sleeping little ones and sleepless teens
Or those who will never wake.
Help us know that in all activities—
Small as in dusting a table
Or large as in preparing the table for dinner—
You are there,
Cheering us on,
Bringing us joy and gladness every day.
Amen.

CHAPTER THREE
Our Response of Faith

What startled the grand-mother were the words.

"Listen up, now! I am not going to tell you again! Your Mama is comin' home soon, and she is not gonna like you!" the grandmother yelled at the child in her care.

But the little girl just looked back at her and didn't move. Her mind was busy with many thoughts. "Mama won't care if I can't do my sister's hair. Anyway, Mama likes it done the new way—like lots of girls have it done. The way they do it in Africa! And Gramma doesn't understand," the ten-year-old thought.

"Hurry up! Your Mama will be tired when she gets here . . . an' we gotta leave for church. Hurry on now . . . get it done, girl!" her grandmother yelled again.

"I can't do it like Mama likes!" the child suddenly blurted out. "She likes it the African way, 'cuz we're glad we're African! And you should be too! It's fine to be African!"

The older woman was startled! Never, ever, in her whole life had a child spoken to her like that. But the problem wasn't that her granddaughter had raised her voice. It wasn't even that she wasn't obeying! What startled the grandmother were the words.

"Sweet Jesus," she thought, "this child is but a child, and she said what she did! Lord, I hear you! Amen, I say, Lord. Amen. Lord, you are a comin'! This child has told me that! Lord, you are a comin'!"

Throughout her life

and until her last ordeal

when Jesus her son

died on the cross,

Mary's faith never wavered.

She never ceased to believe

in the fulfillment of God's

word. And so

the Church venerates in Mary

the purest realization of faith.

CCC, 149

There was a Jewish leader named Nicodemus, who belonged to the party of the Pharisees. One night he went to Jesus and said to him, "Rabbi, we know that you are a teacher sent by God. No one could perform the miracles you are doing unless God were with him." Jesus answered, "I am telling you the truth: no one can see the Kingdom of God without being born again." "How can a grown man be born again?" Nicodemus asked. "He certainly cannot enter his mother's womb and be born a second time!" "I am telling you the truth," replied Jesus, "that no one can enter the Kingdom of God without being born of water and the Spirit. A person is born physically of human parents, but is born spiritually of the Spirit. Do not be surprised because I tell you that you must be born again. The wind blows wherever it wishes; you hear the sound it makes, but you do not know where it comes from or where it is going. It is like that with everyone who is born of the Spirit."

John 3:1-8

Now, Nicodemus was no ordinary person.

This scriptural story demonstrates how God offers the opportunity, the invitation, the glory, and all we need do is say "Yes, Lord!" (Much like the little girl's grandmother did in our family story!)

The story of Nicodemus is one of the most revealing and profound stories in the gospels because rich symbols and ideas fill it to overflowing. The story invites us to understand a great deal about our Catholic faith.

The setting immediately alerts us to the fact that something important is going to happen: a private meeting with Jesus, and, not insignificantly, during the night. Now, Nicodemus was no ordinary person. He was a member of the Jewish ruling body, like our members of Congress. He knew human ways and human power. And what Jesus was doing and saying clearly impressed Nicodemus! Like himself, Jesus must be a man of power. "Perhaps if I could befriend him or connect with him," Nicodemus thought, "I would help myself." (We know that for political people contacts are important!)

Jesus, however, knew what was in this man's heart and the reason for the night visit. Knowing Nicodemus's heart, Jesus told him that what he sought—and it wasn't power—came only from God! In fact, what God offered was vastly different from power, so much so that if Nicodemus truly desired this gift, he would have to be born again.

Nicodemus knew that no one could go back into the womb! Jesus explained that he was not talking about birth in the flesh, but in the Spirit—birth from above. Then, with the gentleness of a caring teacher, he told Nicodemus that he was not alone in his confusion, that faith was as simple and as complex as the wind.

We are not told whether Nicodemus accepted Jesus' offer. However, later in the gospels, after the death of Jesus, Nicodemus appears again, bringing oil and spices for the burial of the crucified Jesus. Perhaps in the end we do know the choice he made.

The grace of faith opens "the eyes of your hearts" (Ephesians 1:18)

CCC, 158

> *Faith is a gift; it is like an unexpected visitor or a surprise telephone call.*

Faith is nothing more nor less than the encounter of love: God's loving invitation to us to become part of God's family and our joyful willingness to accept the invitation. This lies at the heart of what we call conversion. It is a turning of our heart to God. To say "I believe" may sound simple, but it isn't, because "I believe" means "I have faith." And oftentimes understanding what this really means is difficult for us.

Faith comes only from God. It is a gift; it is like an unexpected visitor or a surprise telephone call from a long-lost friend. Its arrival startles us. We did nothing to deserve it or to control it. It simply came to us. And that, in itself, is a little scary. God makes the first move, an absolutely necessary move that has to happen before we can make any human response to God.

In other words, God loves us first, visits us, knocks, and waits for us to open the door. That's the sequence and again that's good news! God seeks us out even though we may show no interest. And our God will keep this up all the days of our life. God never gives up.

But there is a catch here: God makes the first move; we must make the next. And this may be hard to believe, but God is respectful of us and our freedom to decide. God will not force us to respond. We can say yes or no.

God took a decided risk in creating us. God could have made a foolproof system, one guaranteed to work, in which we were unable to say no. But consider, if we had to say yes, if we were programmed to say yes, we could never say it with love. Why? Because the essence of love is the free response of one person to another. Without true love, no deep faith exists within us.

We trust in God

Good common sense.

We're all so careful. We carry umbrellas with us just in case of a sudden rain shower. We protect ourselves with insurance for virtually every aspect of our lives. We plan into the future to avoid its uncertainties. In a word, we want to control everything, often even the people we live with! Leave nothing to doubt! Cover your you-know-what! Don't trust! Leave nothing to God!

As Christians we know that the deeper our faith, the more we place our trust, our very life, in the hands of God, who will not abandon us. This seems easy until we remember our contemporary culture and its powerful influence, which ask us to decrease risk and increase security. Many of those we know will view us as either impractical or foolish when they see us taking the risk of trusting in God's assistance.

Clearly this trust is a complex aspect of our faith. When does leaving our lives open to what God turn into being stupid? When does leaving the future wide open to any possibility translate into irresponsibility?

These are difficult questions. Saint Ignatius supposedly said that we should pray as if everything depends on God and act as if everything depends on us! Thus, the life of faith-filled trust in God holds hands with good common sense and practicality, which are also gifts from God. We must live our faith in actions as well as words.

Faith seeks understanding and goes beyond it

Because God created the universe, we believe that the content of revelation (God in life) cannot contradict the findings of our own senses, nor the findings of genuine science. Faith and reason go together. One of God's greatest creative works was the creation of the human mind and intellect. We must use this gift fully.

The Church may seem to some to be antiscience or even anti-intellectual at certain times. However, its deeper, truer roots encourage us to

Faith is loaded with surprises.

accept our God-given ability to reason and to figure out what this universe is all about. Our acts of reason and our faith help us grasp the deeper meanings of faith and connect this faith with everyday life and ordinary human experience. Recognizing God in life is "revelation" to us!

But faith speaks also of mysteries that go beyond our human capacity to perceive. Some may believe that nothing is beyond a human's intellectual capacity. In the last century, we have experienced great leaps of understanding. In fact, we sometimes think that given the right tools for observation, the right computer, or the right human insight, we can break through all boundaries and know everything!

Scripture scholars describe this belief as the sin of Adam and Eve—the sin of wanting to know as God knows! But our faith reminds us that we can only go so far with our wonderful (yet limited) minds. A barrier may be moved further out as time passes, but the barrier will always be there. We cannot directly see God, nor can we act as if we are God.

This is exactly what happened to Nicodemus. He went as far as his wisdom could carry him. However, Jesus invited Nicodemus to go further. His openness, his willingness to listen and accept the word of Jesus, is at the heart of the act of faith. God's word comes, we listen, and then we seek to understand and accept the truth.

The history of our lives shows hundreds and hundreds of little conversions as we seek, accept, and then proceed ahead on our journey as Christians. The family story that began this chapter is a wonderful example of how we learn and accept new insights.

Much like Jesus and Nicodemus, the little African-American girl opened the eyes of her grandmother through her own knowledge and understanding. The older woman carried a whole set of values from the past. But from somewhere deep within, the grandmother already knew what the little girl told her. The words of the child became, for the grandmother, the sign that God was at work. Thus, a leap of faith!

Faith is loaded with surprises. After describing the resurrection of Jesus, the gospels tell us of his encounters with friends and followers. Two people (some wonder if they were a married couple) walk toward a town called Emmaus. A stranger joins them. The two find themselves talking freely about the amazing events of the last few days. Finally, the three stop for a brief meal, break bread together, and the stranger leaves. Suddenly the two travelers realize who he was—their good friend Jesus, now risen.

Why hadn't they recognized him while they traveled together on the road? Because he had changed; this was the Risen Lord, Christ Jesus. But as they reflect on their feelings while with him that day, they recall how their hearts burned within them. In a sense, something in them told them who he was all along.

That's the way of faith. Jesus told Nicodemus about a deeper dimension of power and life. The grandchild brought her grandmother a new awareness. The capacity for new insight and understanding was within both Nicodemus and the grandmother, but this capacity needed the word of another to bring it out. Our God communicates like that. God uses human means—gestures, conversations, good example, the formal language of the Church, nature, words, and more—to communicate with us. And when we hear or see this as from God, from a power outside ourselves, then faith changes us forever.

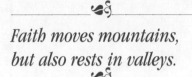

Faith moves mountains, but also rests in valleys.

Our God is a God of everyday life (around the clock), and there are probably hundreds of moments when we listen and hear our God speak to us. We say, "God, I hear you!" and make a leap of faith. Those moments change us forever. Those moments are like the one the grandmother experienced.

Not all moments are as dramatic as those experienced by the grandmother and by Nicodemus. But even less dramatic times, like seeing one of our kids picking dandelions, can bring forth from us a leap of faith. In many and myriad ways, God is visible in the happenings of our daily, ordinary life.

When can we see God?

When we receive a smile from a person in line at the store. *"Lord, I see you!"*

When we meet a courteous driver. *"Lord, I experience you!"*

When we receive an unexpected card from a friend or family. *"Lord, I recognize you!"*

When we share a good-bye kiss with someone who has touched our life but who is going out of it. *"Lord, I miss you."*

In these and in thousands of incidental moments in our life, God steps in and gently blesses us with love.

Faith moves mountains, but faith also rests in valleys, in the daily routines we may overlook. As we continue our journey today, let us decide to look for those whispering moments when God gently says, "Here I am." And perhaps we might respond, "Lord, I hear you."

Let's try to put these ordinary experiences in the landscape of our life. And let us remember them as significant. Through them we leap into faith.

A Psalm

Come, let us praise the Lord!
Let us sing for joy to God, who protects us!
Let us come before him with thanksgiving
and sing joyful songs of praise.
Come, let us bow down and worship him;
let us kneel before the Lord, our Maker!
He is our God; we are the people he cares for,
the flock for which he provides.
Listen today to what he says:
"Don't be stubborn, as your ancestors were at Meribah,
as they were that day in the desert at Massah."

Psalm 95:1, 2, 6–8

The Soft Hearts of Family

Sometimes it's so hard, dear Lord,
To listen for your voice
Because so much is going on.
Sometimes we don't even have time to think!
But we know, God,
You're here when we're busy changing diapers
or tires or bedding or taking the laundry
From the washer to the dryer or the clothesline.
And often,
We sense you when we're fixing supper,
or broken toys,
or hearts.
We know listening is important,
And we do have time
To listen for you as we listen to each other,
As we get up and rush to get out
To school, or work, or some other
Holy place.
And we hear you,
When you come in from school or work
     or some other
Holy place
And reenter our holy space,
Where you live so softly,
In our hearts,
In our hearth,
In our home.
Amen.

CHAPTER FOUR

God Is Revealed as Trinitarian Love

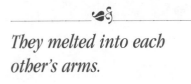

They melted into each other's arms.

He couldn't believe it was happening to him. Finding someone like her. He never imagined she . . . or someone like her . . . even existed on earth!

Now here he sat, waiting for her to get off the plane. His feelings almost overwhelmed him. He could actually hear his heart beating.

And then there she was. The world faded away as their eyes met again. Only he . . . only she . . . existed in all the universe.

They melted into each other's arms, and bodies on fire met in glorious embrace. It was as if each body wanted to pull the other fully inside so they would be one.

Then, when consciousness returned, they let go and, in unison, awkwardly asked, "How are you?" Then laughed in adolescent-style embarrassment.

But they couldn't look away. Their eyes could not get enough of each other.

"God, she's beautiful," he thought.

"Oh, I love him," she thought.

"Are you hungry?" he asked.

"No. I just want to go. Okay?" she answered.

"Okay. Let's go," he replied.

As the sunlight hit them outside, it warmed their bodies even more, and she reached to put her arm through his.

It was then it happened. The rose. In full bloom. Right in front of them by the side of the airport sidewalk. Their eyes met again, and the realization of their common thoughts created a wave of passion between them.

Then they bent down, together, to experience another sweet scent of their God.

Believing in God . . . *means knowing the unity and true dignity of all . . . :* Everyone is made in the image and likeness of God.

CCC, 222, 225

And we ourselves know and believe the love which God
has for us. God is love, and those who live in love live
in union with God and God lives in union with them.

1 John 4:16

*Do we recognize God as
the love between us?*

Two lines from Scripture.
That's all we need here,
yet pages could be and
have been written about
the richness of this
message.

Through our slow, meditative reading of these
words, we connect with one of the most elusive
concepts of our faith. Yet, this concept is also a reality
we humans have in common with all humanity—the
experience of loving and being loved by someone else.

Three words—*God is love*—invite us to embrace the
heart of our faith. These words invite us to understand
the deepest truth of our God—that God's very being is
love. If we allow this idea to replace all our other ideas
of God, ideas incompatible with love, then we have
made a giant leap toward understanding the wonder
of God.

"Those who abide in love, abide in God, and God in
them." Are we in love with someone? Do we abide in
that love? Do we exist with God? Do we recognize and
accept God as the love within and between us and
others?

We all know that we can love in many ways. In fact,
experiencing love is a never-complete and elusive task.
Let's recall here our own experience of love and the
different ways we love. Let's think for a moment of

those people in our life right now—children, parents, friends. Then we want to remember those persons who are part of the memories we have of loving and being loved. Our God is this love. The couple in the story that begins this chapter feel that strong love and recognize God in their love through the symbol of love—the rose.

Their love cannot be contained within just the two of them. It swells within them and breaks forth into the world around them. It can, in very important ways, change the world. Real love has that kind of power.

In the Church we experience the power of God's love. And we understand that power because we have experienced the love of our family. In that love—the love of our family, we know the reality of God, who *is* love.

> *"Now this is the Catholic faith: We worship one God in the Trinity and the Trinity in unity . . . for the person of the Father is one, the Son is another, the Holy Spirit's another." (Athanasian Creed)*
>
> CCC, 266

Through the person and life of Jesus, God revealed a new name.

Most Catholics know something about what we call the Trinity. We've heard that this term means three Persons in one God—God the loving Father, God the redeeming Son, and God the enlivening Spirit. But few of us spend time thinking about this official teaching of the Church. We simply accept it as a great mystery.

This simple acceptance, with no attempt to understand the mystery, is sad. A teaching that lays out the fullest possible meaning of what we call existence, just might be meaningful for most of us!

Learning that God is, that God loves intensely and passionately, is joy for the journey. And God has always been that way. Always! And will always be that way.

For us this means that by coming into God's family, we are given a real share in both God's life and God's love. To understand this, we must first learn a little about the history of God's relationship with humanity.

The first name of God

Names are very important. A parent carefully chooses a name for a new child. We all delight when someone remembers our name and calls us by name. Our name singles us out from the crowd. We change from being a thing or an object to being a person, a unique being.

In a similar way, the religions of ancient time were distinguished by the names given to their god or gods. Most of us have heard the story of Moses. Born as a slave in Egypt, Moses rose to prominence in Pharaoh's court.

At that time, God's interaction with people seemed far more apparent than we experience today. For example, once God appeared to Moses in the form of a burning bush. The fire burning the bush did not consume it. This fire drew its energy from the presence of God, whose love is steadfast and never ending, whose love fulfills without destroying.

From the burning bush, God invited Moses to bring the Israelites out of Egypt and into a land of abundance, a land flowing with milk and honey. God also gave Moses a new description of God—Yahweh. This new name for our loving God means "I am who am." Some translations say it means "I am whom I will be."

What is the meaning of this unusual name? How does it tell us something about God?

The name *Yahweh* tells us that God is present both now and in the future. As God revealed this name, Moses learned that the Israelites would escape slavery, seek freedom, find abundance. And while their journey would be arduous and perhaps even dangerous, God would always and ever be with them. God is thus revealed as a God who frees, saves, and enriches—now and forever.

Up until the time of Jesus, the name *Yahweh* was the proper name for God, revealed through the First, or Old, Testament. The name was a great one. And then, through the person and life of Jesus, God revealed a new name.

The God of Jesus

Jesus called God "Abba"—Daddy.

We can think about the divine aspect of Jesus from two perspectives. We can accept though faith that Jesus himself was God. But we can also learn about God through the way Jesus relates to God. He called God "Abba."

This name for God is taken directly from the family life Jesus knew as a young Jewish boy. This is probably what he called Joseph, his foster father. We know for certain that Jesus used this word when he prayed. Thus, he called God "Abba"—Daddy.

The name *Abba* can fill us with feelings of closeness and love, of familiarity and trust. When Jesus taught us to begin our prayer with "Our Father" (our Abba), he invited us into a similar relationship with God, a relationship of trusting love.

Jesus' relationship with his Abba was so strong that he could trust and thus say yes to the wishes of God. This relationship, filled with trusting love, allowed Jesus to submit freely to death on the cross. That same loving relationship brought forth the resurrection.

Moreover, that loving relationship continued when the Spirit descended upon Jesus' followers and filled them with God's love. Again, the symbol used by God was fire, burning this time over the heads of the disciples. With God's love enflaming their hearts, they journeyed beyond Jerusalem to bring the message of this unconditional love to others.

Is the energy of that type of burning love familiar to you? That love moves us to get up and go, as the apostles did. We want to be with others, to celebrate, to tell others about the love.

The Trinity of God

The New Testament provided the newborn Church with a foundation for its understanding of God as three persons. But a clear expression of this belief in

God challenges our imagination.

the Trinity was not soon in coming to the Church. In fact, close to three hundred years passed before a Church council agreed on an adequate description of the Trinity!

Thinking about more than one Person within God challenges our imagination. Central to this belief is that the three Persons of God are complete and equal, although different. And they are so connected that they do not act separately from one another. They abide in one another.

Our human minds cannot grasp or picture what this inner life of God is like. But our deepest experience of human love gives us an inkling of this life. For example, in the reunion story at the beginning of this chapter, we witnessed a couple deeply, passionately in love with each other. They have been apart and during the separation they felt an emptiness, a hole right in the center of their lives. They wanted to be together, to see each other, to hold each other, and to allow the energy of their love to flow freely between them.

Their meeting was a sacred moment, connected with God's love, because we are made in the image of God and God is love. God, then, is part of their love. God is at the center of their relationship. God is between them!

In summary, we can suggest the following ideas as important and meaningful.

God is more than one Person. God is diverse. What holds God together, so to speak, is the love between the Persons of God. This love is eternal and the motive for God to create reality outside God's own self. In addition, the fact of the Trinity suggests that God is not lonely. God has no need to create anyone or anything. Yet God creates outside Godself. Why? Just because of love. God freely and intentionally chooses to create everything and everyone—unique and precious, never to be created again.

Further, all creation, but particularly personal life in creation, has a special relationship to God. God hopes we will abide in love. God deeply desires that we will abide in God.

Finally, we can now see why the family is such a holy place, a sacred community. When the family is a community of love, however small a spark this love might be, it truly shows that it is the dwelling place of our God. And God is very happy in our midst.

Is love worth the effort?

God displayed a sense of humor in creating us. We are a strange and wonderful mix of needs, wants, and desires. Some of the most pleasurable experiences of our life happen when we are with other people. And some of the most hurtful moments of our life also happen when we are with other people. We were made to love, but what makes life so difficult is just that—love! A French philosopher once said that hell is other people. On some days we would agree with him; on other days, we'd run him out of town!

Living in community, rubbing shoulders with family members, coworkers, and even strangers, can be invigorating and draining—and sometimes this changes from minute to minute.

True love can be difficult and demanding. True love involves risks and the letting go of control. Is love worth the effort?

We can pack all kinds of things for our life's journey, but sometimes we carry so much that the suitcase becomes a burden. If we are to go on, we must lighten our load; we must keep only the items we truly need for the journey.

Our faith tells us that the only thing we need is love. At journey's end, even faith and hope become unnecessary. Thus, the down-to-earth person will make the right choices. We will separate what's good (but not really important) from that which is really important . . . and good too!

What are we carrying that is not love? What might we need to unpack and gently lay aside?

A Psalm

You are praised by people everywhere,
and your fame extends over all the earth.
You rule with justice;
let the people of Zion be glad!
You give right judgments;
let there be joy in the cities of Judah!

Psalm 48:10–11

The Fire of Family

Sometimes in the middle of the night
We hear sirens, and we feel fear
And ask ourselves or another,
"Wonder if there's a fire."

We really don't want an answer.
We just wonder with a little bit of fear.
Then we fall back to sleep
And fire is *Fear.*

Other times we sit by a campfire
With marshmallows or other yummy things
And warm ourselves
While laughter flows and stories are told
And fire is *Fun.*

And sometimes we watch a candle
In the center of a table
Adorned with best cloth, utensils, and food.
We pray in thanksgiving

For one another and the food.
And the fire in our midst is
You. Amen.

CHAPTER FIVE

God's Good Creation and Humanity's Sin

The wonder of the universe calmed their perspiring bodies.

The night was so hot. Nobody in the house was able to sleep. Even the dog was wandering around. "Daddy, I'm hot," the littlest blurted out from the bed next to his.

"I know, Pedro. Take your shirt off and you'll feel better," he replied.

"It's off, but I'm still hot," the six-year-old whined.

He got up, reached for a nearby magazine, went over to his son's bed, and began to fan him. "There. Is that better?" the sweltering dad asked.

"I'm hot too," came another voice.

"Me too," came the chorus from other spaces in the apartment.

He heaved a deep sigh. "Okay, everybody, get up, grab your pillow, and follow me!" he commanded. On his way out the door, he grabbed the old tarp and, together with his five offspring (and a lot of questions), climbed the steps to the roof of the building.

Immediately on coming out onto the rough asphalt, he felt better. Then, to the amazed faces of his children, the industrious father spread the tarp, told them to pick a space for their pillow, and lay down.

Getting the idea, the already-feeling-better children followed his lead. Soon the whole family covered the tarp with bronze bodies, much like a painting.

When he put his head back against the tarp, he saw them—millions and millions of tiny stars, unbound from their smog by the nighttime wind. The panorama before him looked as if the top of the sky had been pulled back to reveal the heavens beyond.

Rarely did they see this. And almost in unison the children said, "Oo . . . oo . . . oo!"

All was quiet. At least up there, on top of the world, because the noises of the city could be heard only if one really wanted to hear them.

But no one did. And no one was really any cooler, either, due to the hot asphalt. But they were content. The wonder of the universe calmed their perspiring bodies.

Very soon he heard the sound of his children sleeping. Added to the silence of the stars, the sound reminded him of symphony rehearsals he heard when he cleaned the concert hall.

However, the sounds of the music of the universe and his children sleeping were much, much more beautiful.

The Creator is a source of wisdom and freedom, of joy and confidence.

CCC, 301

In the beginning, when God created the universe, the earth was formless and desolate. The raging ocean that covered everything was engulfed in total darkness, and the Spirit of God was moving over the water. Then God commanded, "Let there be light"—and light appeared.

Genesis 1:1–3

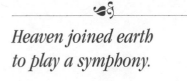

Heaven joined earth to play a symphony.

The image of darkness into light is a great way of describing something. What one of us hasn't lain awake as a child (or as an adult) and wished for the light? To illuminate our lives is a necessary, natural need. Without light, we can't see. In a sense, whatever is present around us, familiar or not, is a formless wasteland unless we can see it. Light must come for order to take shape around us.

Families use the image of light all the time. We use light as a way to describe thought: "It dawned on me!" "Suddenly, a light went on inside of me!" "When will you see the light?" "Lighten up!"

And who among us hasn't had an experience similar to that of the father in our story? We were suddenly changed by the experience of simply laying our head back and having the sky open before us. The stars, the moon, call forth a sense of awe within us.

The father felt peace because his children were finally comfortable enough to sleep (a triumph enough in a parent's life!). But the magnificence of the heavens above transformed this moment into a spiritual experience. All became a new creation for him, as heaven joined earth to play a symphony unlike any he'd ever heard—the silence of the stars mingled with the sounds of his sleeping children.

From the darkness of not being able to provide comfort for his children in the holiness of his own home, he rose to seek what he hoped was relief and found yet another gift of creation.

Holy are the moments of our lives when darkness becomes light.

God cares for all,

from the least things

to the great events

of the world and its history.

CCC, 303

The Creator was a maker, a builder, an artisan, a visionary.

Let's think about how far back in life we can remember. To when we were five? Three? Even earlier? Most likely when we bring up our earliest conscious memory, we see ourselves in a scene in which we are awake. The point is that at some time in the past, each of us woke up and realized that we were here! Someone turned on the lights.

Suddenly, we began to wonder, Who am I? Where am I? What's going on around here? These are among our first important spiritual questions. They dawn in us as our mind wakes up.

Sooner or later, we add other important queries to our list. Where did I come from? How did all this begin? Finally, we seek explanations to move us beyond what is immediately present. The question Who did this? becomes part of our journey. A quest for our God. This time, the Creator.

Stories of creation

When we explain an experience, we sometimes start by saying, "In the beginning." Genesis, the first book of the Old Testament, starts with these words and tells us about our beginning.

The accounts of creation found in Genesis use the words and images of the people of those days, just as our writings reflect our own experience. Nevertheless, these ancient stories exhibit many timeless and insightful truths. Creation moved from chaos to order, from darkness to light, from lifeless things to life-filled creatures, and from nonhumans to humans.

The process of creation is presented as a gentle process. It was not violent or disruptive. It was built up with one part (day) leading to the next. It implies a plan, a wisdom that was unfolding as God placed each new element into the whole. Creation was effortless; the Creator simply thought about what was next and whatever that thought was, it came to be.

Perhaps the most important aspect of the biblical creation stories is this: All that God created was good! Creation was not divided into good parts and bad parts, holy parts and profane parts. It held together in a oneness, a place for everything and everything within its place. The Creator was a maker, a builder, an artisan, a visionary.

And one final amazing fact: The raw material for creating was nothing! Absolutely nothing. Totally from scratch. And this in itself was tremendously significant. For God? Not really. But for the created, especially for the masterpieces made on the last working day. Because on that day, in God's image, we were created as male and female. And that was good, very good!

Creation—God's gift of love

God created us more to play than to work, more to feast than to fast.

Strong in Catholic tradition is the belief that creation is connected to redemption. For after the entrance of sin into our world there followed the response of Jesus' life, death, and resurrection, which saved us for God and eternal life.

Creation came first; redemption followed. Redemption completes creation. Catholic theology notes that the first sin of humanity (we name it original sin) tarnished humanity and creation, but did not destroy them.

Both creation and redemption are expressions of God's love. God created the universe for us; Jesus died and God raised him to new life for us. Always, always, God is for us. Creation is a celebration of God's goodness and love. We acknowledge that fact whenever we celebrate life in its fullness, whenever we respond in a way equal to the magnificence and beauty of the gift. We are a people who are deeply grateful.

In Genesis, God rests after creation; God takes a break. But God does not leave creation to go on willy-nilly without the presence of Love, without the presence of God. We believe that if God were to withdraw presence and support for what was created—only for an instant—the universe and all that is in it would collapse and disappear into its original condition: nothingness!

So God remains involved in maintaining that which was right from the beginning. When we speak of God's providence (God's ongoing direction of creation), we focus on God's love as revealed in Scripture and in Tradition and on God's presence and guidance in our personal life. God is present to us, but God does not violate or overstep our freedom. God's love is lavishly bestowed on us, but we can choose to accept or reject it.

Earlier we reflected on the family stories of Noah and Abraham. God was part of their family life. And while the experiences of their families with God held important historical meaning for those particular families and symbolism for us, they were not the only families led by God.

How do we know this? Simply because we believe that God does not play favorites! God is the God of all. God is not the God of a few or the God of only one kind of people or time or nation or particular religious tradition.

A good explanation of the doctrine of creation will challenge any notion of a Catholic God, a Protestant God, a Muslim God, or a God of nonbelievers. God is one; there is only one God, and God is deeply present to all of creation.

God created us more to play than to work, more to feast than to fast, more to smile than to cry, and more for joy in our hearts than anger in our actions. Doing less is an insult to the generosity of the Creator. Creation is still happening, but no longer is creation the solo act of God. God has made us partners in this great undertaking. Together we continue creation. How? In many ways. But one we all know about is the birth of a child. After our child is born, we continue forever and a day to nurture and love that child. Thus, we continue—with God—to create.

Sin enters an imperfect world

Even Jesus needed to learn.

What a wonderful moment it is when we realize that each of us is imperfect, particularly in the sense of being incomplete or not finished yet! Perfectionism is a terrible human condition. It implies that one needs to be godlike, without any fault. The truth of God's good creation is that we're more like raw material than a finished product.

Let's take the family and its role as provider for its young, When we enter the world, a parent does not expect us to recite Shakespeare in the crib, nor even to sleep through the night. All of us learn a realistic approach to creation when we accept the reality of not being able to do all or be all. One cannot give what one does not have.

Even Jesus needed to learn how to saw off the end of a board in a straight line. Joseph never took the child Jesus into his carpenter's shop and said, "Now I know that you already know how to make a drop-leaf table so I will leave you alone. And since you also know the future, I would like something from the early colonial period!"

When the ancients told their story that became the Book of Genesis, they sought to explain humanity as they saw it. They recognized in those around them some traits that made them like Yahweh; they also saw humanity's limitations, ways that made them unlike God. To illustrate these limitations, or boundaries, the ancient writers used the symbolic tree with the forbidden fruit. To choose this fruit was to turn from God's loving will. To go against this desire for our own wholeness was to sin.

Of course we know that Adam and Eve made their choice and departed from the garden. Turning from God, they met the burden of work. The labor of childbirth and the labor of the fields suddenly became part of being human. And, as the Book of Genesis goes on to tell, the families of their descendants continued to choose evil, to violate God's law, and to feel the effect of their own sins. The fact that Adam and Eve's choice affected their descendants is an additional piece of bad news! And we are some of those descendants!

All humanity is constantly faced with choices and decisions. The failure to live life in the garden, the way God invited us to live, is told over and over again in Scripture. We find this choice to turn from the delights of God (the love, freely given, of God) in our homes, in our neighborhoods, in our work places, and even in our churches. We hear the results of this choice on TV each night and read about them in our daily newspapers.

We experience the full horror of sin as we become both the victims and the doers of evil. The victims often become the victimizers. But God does not allow the sin of humans to be the last word. Jesus' resurrection is the last word.

Thus, creation is aimed toward success and happiness, not failure. Catholic tradition has described the sin, the choice, of Adam and Eve as a happy fault. Why?

Because it brought about the coming of Jesus as our Savior. All creation—even its failures—is filled with the goodness of God, for from these deaths came the resurrection.

God created all sorts of beings. We treasure trees and plants, birds and beasts, sky and stars, and angels! The Church teaches that angels are spirits without bodies. However, contrary to all the pictures we see of them, there is no scriptural reference to wings. The word *angel* simply means "messenger of God." These mysterious beings are messengers of God's care and love for us.

Many families have a strong belief in guardian angels who guard each member of the family. Children often say a prayer to their angel to protect them through the night. This is a reminder that our God is a God of the home and the family—especially of children.

The secular world often laughs at, denigrates, or denies our belief in angels and even in God. Yet a true understanding of the God of creation leaves us with a sense of God's presence from the beginning until this very moment. Thus, we find that we must believe in this God who loves us so prodigally, so extravagantly, so excessively. This God who reaches out to us in every moment of every day.

We find God on the high mountaintops and in the dark valleys of our life, on the dry land and in the churning ocean, in crawling ants and trumpeting elephants, on the distant moon and in the depths of the earth, and even in the whisper of the wind and the gurgle of water. And we find God in surprising places such as the enjoyment of sports and the miracles of technology. Such is the wonder of creation!

We find God in the tiny hand of a newborn.

With this chapter, we enter into the wonder of our beginning with the very first part of our Creed, "I believe in God, the Father almighty, creator of heaven and earth."

What a profound statement that is! Even to stand as we say "I believe" is a wonderful response to our Creator! In truth, we are saying, "Yes, Lord, I am one of those you have created. I believe it and know it!"

All the heavens must wave flags when we do that. A family probably feels this way when a child crosses that long platform in the high school gym and puts a hand out for the diploma. Throats choke; cameras flash; a little group of cheers can be heard from somewhere in the upper right-hand corner of the crowded gymnasium. Such is the importance of one of us saying "I believe . . ."

Creation is on our mind when we begin the Creed. We may think of the natural cycle of the seasons, the miracle of what a seed can do in fertile soil, the magnitude of the plains and jungles of Africa, the majesty of the Rocky Mountains, or the mystery of the blue water of the ocean.

But we also, in thinking of creation, think of God. We look and find God in the tiny hand of a newborn, the frail body of an old person, the wagging tail of a dog, the tired mom picking up her child from day care, the couple holding hands, or the proud Little Leaguer who just scored a run. In each, we see the creative love of God.

The next time we see one of these wonders of creation, each of us might consider whispering to ourself, "I believe." Each time we see one of these wonders, or a hundred million other creations like them.

A Psalm

But the joy that you have given me
is more than they will ever have
with all their grain and wine.
When I lie down, I go to sleep in peace;
you alone, O Lord, keep me perfectly safe.

Psalm 4:7–8

Family Soup Psalm

God of heaven and earth, stars and moon,
Nourish us with your creation.
With that organic soup,
Which has been cooking all along.
Give us sights
Of smiling faces and soiled fingers.
Give us sounds
Of ringing phones and baby cries.
Give us tastes
Of leftover pizza and salty tears.
Give us smells
Of baking bread and musty closets.
Give us touches
Of sticky kisses and awkward hugs.
Light the darkness when we fail to see each other's
    goodness,
Especially those who live with us and next to us,
As we bear each other's burdens
And the burden of each other.
As we lie down
Seeking that place of peaceful rest
Where we rest in you.
Amen.

CHAPTER SIX

The Incarnation: God as Fully Human

Sometimes a baby even came back to her.

The baby was ready, and so was she—at least physically. But she was never ready for the emotional aspect of giving up a child.

Still, it was time. They'd had the little boy for almost a year now, longer than most. And she was never sure if the pain of letting go of the little one would get easier or harder. She just knew the pain would be with her.

As the years of being a foster mother had come and gone, so had many, many little ones. She kept careful count and had pictures, but more than anything else, she had held each of these babies (always babies) in her heart.

Now the time had come, once again, to say good-bye. Tons and tons of cloth and disposable diapers were long gone. Hours and hours of bathing, feeding, rocking, soothing, and playing were over. At least for little Donald.

Hopefully his new parent would do the same. (Hopefully.) She always wondered and prayed that each baby would be given the same love she'd given each child. Sometimes she found out. Often she didn't.

Sometimes a baby even came back to her. For whatever reason, being with the parent didn't work out. For some, these were "disposable" babies.

She piled the two of them into the car. The other baby was just newborn and oblivious to the event. He just needed a whole lot of love to get him going in this world. Pat had not hesitated when they called to see if she'd take him. After all, she'd raised five of her own.

The afternoon went well. The transition plan for Donald had progressed well, and the new family and he were used to each other. So this day wasn't much different. (How do you say good-bye to somebody who calls you "Mama"?)

She got her coat on. Intrigued with new toys, Donald ignored her. So she just went over and picked him up, as she often did. The child looked at her as usual, with a "What's up, Ma?" look in his eyes.

She hugged him close, and only to herself and her God, she said, "I love you, Donald." A peck on the cheek and the ritual of handing him to his new parent. Then she said her other good-byes, gathered up the other little one, and headed for the car.

Cheerios strewn on his empty car seat brought the inevitable tears. So she took a moment to compose herself before starting the car. Her heart ached. Saying yes to the tearing out of a piece of her heart was always so hard. "Yes, Lord," she said out loud. "Yes, Lord. Yes." And she started the car.

> *Jesus of Nazareth, born a Jew of a daughter of Israel . . . , a carpenter by trade. . . .*
>
> CCC, 423

The Holy Spirit was with him and had assured him that he would not die before he had seen the Lord's promised Messiah. Led by the Spirit, Simeon went into the Temple. When the parents brought the child Jesus into the Temple to do for him what the law required, Simeon took the child in his arms and gave thanks to God: "Now, Lord, you have kept your promise, and you may let your servant go in peace. With my own eyes I have seen your salvation, which you have prepared in the presence of all people."

Luke 2:25–31

Happiness and sadness exist side by side.

We are born, and we die. Two separate events. Both are part of the miracle of life. Both sometimes bleed into each other. The foster mom brought her foster child to his new family. The child was born into the new family at the same moment he died in his foster family. "Good-bye" was connected with "Hello." In the case of Jesus, he departs heaven, and as the New Testament says, he emptied himself and was born into Mary.

Another aspect of both accounts is that happiness and sadness exist side by side. Certainly happiness is the dominant feeling for most of us in birth. But with Mary, with the foster mom, and maybe even with God, a profound sadness fills the birth too. Later will come the suffering of Jesus, a deep and painful suffering. The suffering of God.

Faith invites us to explore the deeper meaning of events and persons. The Incarnation of God calls for deep reflection. It challenges our mind. Why would God want to become human? Why would any of us want to be a foster parent, knowing in advance how close we will get to the infant, the child, or the teen, and how sad we will be when we have to give her or him up?

When Mary realized something of what was going on, she became afraid. Visits from God can do that. So can phone calls from social workers in the middle of the night: "There is a three-month-old little girl at the crisis center. Can you come?"

In ordinary, everyday life, a woman learns that she is pregnant; a man learns that he is to be a father. How to they respond? With fear? Worry? Joy? Gratitude? All these emotions?

Brand-new possibilities fill the horizon when new life happens. When something new enters the world, everything and everyone already there is somehow affected. And what if that which was new was really God? Then we must be alert; we must be on guard, because when this most unexpected possibility happens, when God comes to be with us as one of us, anything might be possible!

> *[Jesus] is truly the Son of God who,*
>
> *without ceasing to be God and Lord,*
>
> *became a man, our brother.*
>
> CCC, 469

Wonder is always the beginning of wisdom.

When we mull over the Incarnation (God made human), we usually end up with more questions than answers. Those who find this truth reasonable probably fail to grasp its dramatic and profound meaning. We can accept a belief or teaching of our Church too easily and too early and stop short of its deeper truth. When we simply memorize the words or recite expressions or formulas of Christian faith without thought or feeling, we may be accepting only the wrapping and not the gift.

A Danish philosopher once stated that we should be horrified by the notion of God's Incarnation. For instance, why did it happen then instead of now? Why did it happen there instead of here? And even more, why would God want to be reduced or compromised by spending time here on earth? Does God not have better things to do? The philosopher suggested that the doctrine of the Incarnation is ridiculous.

This philosopher's honest questions challenge us to confront a fuller meaning of the mystery of the Incarnation. The best orientation to our faith (and our whole life for that matter) is wonder, a feeling we readily accept in children but often consider childish for adults. The wonder years are for kids! Once you learn about things, you feel no wonder; instead, you know assurance and certainty.

Yet what if Albert Einstein never wondered? Many of us suspect that the artistic work of a Rembrandt or a Grandma Moses began first with the look of wonder at an object or person. And what about the wonder in parents as they sit numbly at the college graduation of one of their children? Wonder is always the beginning of deep wisdom and insight. It is also the doorway to a deep and fulfilling knowledge of our faith.

Jesus Christ is fully human

Born to know; ready to grow.

To those with whom Jesus walked and talked and sang songs the fact that he was human would not be a surprise. Obviously he was human! He looked like one of us; he seemed to think like one of us; he expressed emotions like us. He ate and drank each day; he had to wash from time to time; he probably sneezed and caught a cold, and when he went from one town to the next, he probably used the ordinary means of transportation for that time—his feet!

While Jesus was kind and loving, he could also be feisty when the occasion invited this response. He enjoyed the simple pleasures of life, especially with his friends, and he was capable of both deep joy and profound sadness. He laughed and he cried, suffered and died. He was indeed one of us.

And although he was gifted with amazing intellectual understanding, Jesus still had to learn. Who's to say that he did not acquire his deep knowledge of the Jewish Scriptures from his parents—Mary and Joseph? Did Peter, his friend and follower, teach Jesus how to land a big fish? Did Jesus, in turn, repay Peter's generosity by teaching him how to fish for people? Who taught Jesus how to be sensitive to women? To strangers? To children? To sinners? To the downtrodden and over-looked members of his society? Are we to assume that Jesus came into this world with everything he needed to know already within him?

No, he was just like us. Born to know; ready to grow. A good person, we might say. One we could trust; one we could count on.

Jesus Christ is fully divine

Now comes the hard part. Jesus was also God. Not just like God, nor close to God, nor a representation of God. No. The real God.

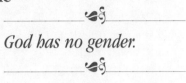

God has no gender.

Eventually he would be known as the Second Person of the Trinity, the Son of God. Note, however, and this is no simple matter, that when we use human language to describe God, the language always has another, deeper meaning. Human language limits us when we describe God. We have only human metaphors and images to use as we try to grasp the mysterious truth of God.

So when we say "the Son of God," we do not mean this in a biological sense. Nor does this mean that the Son is male. God has no gender. The term simply means that God the Son related to God the Father by some kind of generation or progression. In other words, one comes from the other but is not separate from the other, but the same. And their relationship has always been and will always be.

The doctrine of the Incarnation affirms the following: God the Son, existing as God from all time with all power, unites God with human nature. The divine nature of Jesus does not dissolve or overpower his humanity; nor does his humanity reduce or weaken his divinity. The two natures are joined in perfect harmony.

And because in the person of Jesus these two natures unite, they are joined as if they are one reality. This is very good news for us! What a wonderful way to know God—through someone we can understand and relate to—to another who is truly human!

At the beginning of John's gospel, we read that "the Word was made flesh." This summary of the Incarnation uses symbolic language. The *Word* is a rich concept meaning the "idea or wisdom or thought" became flesh.

(Remember we're still in the arena of metaphors—images.)

For *flesh* in his original writing, John used another Greek word with a rich meaning. The word refers to that which is earthy, the soft part of humans, or, sometimes, the part of ourselves of which we are least proud.

So what's the point, we might ask? Well, John's gospel attempts to join that which the readers of those days would consider the most spiritual or heavenly aspect of reality (the Word) with the most earthy or basic part of reality (the flesh). High with low, Creator with creation. In Jesus we find, then, the fullness of all reality.

Jesus is fully for us

If we plunge into Jesus, we find living waters.

What was the reason for the Incarnation? Why did God become human? So that humans could become like God! We are born humans, but we are adopted into the family of God. And while this language is symbolic, it is also concrete and real.

God wants to communicate the mystery of love, which is the foundation of the universe (including each of us). What better way to do this than by dwelling among us and showing us how to love!

God communicates to us in our way—by using our language and our gestures. Jesus invites us to look at him, watch his moves, listen to his parables and ordinary conversations. All his actions and words contain more than we might assume. In Jesus, God is with us—day in and day out, in the ups and downs of living life, both in and outside of family.

Jesus was and is God. So how does our God behave when with us? As a king? A president? A prime minister?

A CEO? A celebrity? We know the answer. None of the above. In the language of Scripture, Jesus comes as a servant, a caring person whose primary concern is the good of others. Jesus loves more deeply and more totally than any other person who has ever lived on this earth. Or anywhere.

Let's think back to the questions raised by the philosopher at the beginning of this chapter. He suggested that the Incarnation was ridiculous. Yet, suppose what we believe is really true. Then what? Well, if God really did come to dwell among us, the one God who is the Creator of all, then finding out about this wonderful mystery might be a good idea. The richness and importance of the Incarnation invites our serious thought and our prayer.

True, this mystery is beyond our ability to fully comprehend. But if we plunge deeper and deeper into the depths of Jesus' humanity and divinity, then we find living waters.

Mary, the mother of Jesus

Mary is a gutsy lady! The gospels describe her willingness to participate in the Incarnation as no small thing. She needed massive

Jesus was born of Mary, a human.

courage to go against her culture and become a pregnant unmarried woman. And she did this willingly! She had a choice.

We can imagine the anxiety the angel's message must have created within her. However, she embraced God's will. Taking a deep breath, Mary said yes. She accepted God's invitation to walk through an open door, trusting, but not knowing, that there was a space beyond the doorway where she could safely step! And there was.

Jesus was born of Mary, a human. Her pregnancy was probably very normal. No prenatal anything, except probably women taking care of women. She probably got sick in the morning. She probably worried about telling her mother and father. And then, at some point, Joseph, to whom she was betrothed (a deeper commitment than engagement), who needed to know.

Scripture tells us of the pain and anxiety Joseph then endured as he tried to decide what he should do. Time passed; they married; they prepared for the birth of a child. All of this is not unlike what some families go through today. Normal human kinds of happenings— joy and pain. Ups and downs.

Mary's sanctity was fashioned within the family. As a unwed pregnant teenager, as a married woman, later as widow, a single mom. Still later, she became a foster mother to John, whom Jesus gave to her as he died. Mary's holiness came from her humanness. Her holiness came out of human struggle.

While we can say that Jesus, no doubt, probably resembled Mary in his physical appearance, she, even more, resembled him in the way she lived a life of love.

Jesus is Mary's only son, but her spiritual motherhood extends to all. . . .

CCC, 501

Many of our major holidays are related to Jesus.

The word *Incarnation* is hardly a household word. Many of us have never really understood its meaning, so we avoid using it. However, we do understand the celebration of Christmas. Christmas is the most important family celebration! We can recount story after story of how our family did this or our family did that at Christmastime. We can remember pain and joy. Most married couples can recall their first few Christmases together, trying to combine two different family ways of "doing Christmas."

We know in our hearts that on this day, the people, the food, the presents are all saying something to us. This day is special, very special. It is about our God connecting with us. And slowly, during our life, we come to appreciate the day, the feast, and our God who made Christmas possible.

So we really do know the Incarnation! We may not know the official word, but we celebrate the coming of Jesus. The celebration speaks to us. That's why celebrations are so important. They can be fun, but they teach. They separate us from our daily routine.

The same can be said for many other celebrations. Our family calendar is connected with the Church's calendar. Think of the ways we celebrate and relive the life of Jesus throughout the year. Many of our major holidays (the word *holiday* is derived from *holy days*) are related to Jesus: New Year's Day, Valentine's Day, Easter, Halloween, Thanksgiving. even Saint Patrick's Day!

We know the story of Jesus! The foster mom in our opening story expresses a love that serves life. Mary does the same. The Incarnation is not an exception to what God intended to happen every day; rather it is at the heart of what happens every day. God's love becomes human. First in Jesus and now in us.

A Psalm

Roar, sea, and every creature in you;
sing, earth, and all who live on you!
Clap your hands, you rivers;
you hills, sing together with joy before the Lord,
because he comes to rule the earth.
He will rule the peoples of the world
with justice and fairness.   *Psalm 98: 7–9*

A Psalm of Reunion and Reconciliation

ummertime
And the livin' is different.
Special time, family time
For retying the knots
Pulled loose by words and touches not made.
Strung out by living further than a stone's throw
Home to home.
Gathered families.
From distant places
From river towns and mountain hamlets
They come.
Cousins, grandfolks, uncles, sisters, and more
All connected (somewhat) by invisible
Memories still alive
And still being told.
Who's here? Who's not?
It makes a difference who comes
And who does not.
It makes all the difference.
For any one
This time
May be the one who brings exactly
The right word
The right move
Needed by this family
To be again.
Amen.

CHAPTER SEVEN
The Life and Death of Jesus

Four kids and no job.

The crying of his little girl woke him. She was two cots over, between her two brothers. He forced himself up and went around Tommy's cot to her.

Her chest was congested; her nose running; her face flushed. So the tired father grabbed the handkerchief out of his wrinkled pants and wiped her little face.

"Sh . . . h . . . h," he gently coaxed her. "Daddy's here. You're okay. Do you want some water?"

"Uh-huh," she answered.

He picked up the little three-year-old and went to the shelter's kitchen. Everybody in the whole place was asleep, he supposed, except him. The world slept, and he was lucky to have found beds again.

"Funny," he thought, as he tipped the glass to her mouth. "I feel so good when I find a place for us— especially if it's for more than one night—but some- where in the middle of the night, probably because I've had a little sleep, the terrible feeling comes back."

As he held his little girl and rocked her back and forth in his arms, the father felt alone and abandoned. His thoughts rambled: "I wish I could get us out of this. Who would've thought this'd happen to me? Four kids and no job. But I won't give them up . . . I'd rather die than do that. We'll make it . . . I know we will."

He walked back toward their cots and laid his daughter down. As he watched her fall to sleep, he found hope growing within himself. "Maybe this place I'll see tomorrow will give me some work."

And then, remembering the days behind him, he realized, "People just don't trust you when you don't have an address. And no matter how I try and keep us clean, people always stare and I can feel their thoughts. I wish they knew what it's like."

Lying down on his own cot and staring at the ceiling, the father sighed and then his thoughts grew a little dark. "Sometimes I feel like nobody cares. They just go to sleep each night. They don't even realize how lucky they are to have beds. And I struggle to find a bed each night for my little girl."

Shutting his eyes tight he cried out as quietly as he could, "Oh, God! Can't you help me? Can't you?"

During the greater part of his life Jesus shared the condition of the vast majority of human beings; a daily life without greatness, a life of manual labor.

CCC, 531

They came to a place called Gethsemane, and Jesus said to his disciples, "Sit here while I pray." He took Peter, James, and John with him. Distress and anguish came over him, and he said to them, "The sorrow in my heart is so great that it almost crushes me. Stay here and keep watch." He went a little farther on, threw himself on the ground, and prayed that, if possible, he might not have to go through that time of suffering. "Father," he prayed, "my Father! All things are possible for you. Take this cup of suffering away from me. Yet not what I want, but what you want."

Mark 14:32–36

Even Jesus asked to have his pain taken away.

The above scriptural account took place the night before Jesus died. And like most of us when we or our loved ones are facing a terrible crisis, even Jesus asked God, whom he addressed as his loving parent, to take away his pain. He sought release from what he was going through and what awaited him.

Like Jesus, the young father in our story is troubled and distressed by his situation in life. And just as Jesus felt abandoned by his closest friends (who fell asleep even though he needed them), the father feels abandoned too. The world in which he lives, in which he struggles to provide for his children, in which he even has to scrounge for a safe bed for them each night, is asleep to him, unaware of his need to provide for his children.

He knows millions of people are safely sleeping in beds that await them each night in comfortable homes. Most probably they have extra beds and bedrooms and more food for their pets than he has for his children.

Each day he faces a sort of death without anyone who really cares if he and his children live or die. Yet, like Jesus, he moves toward acceptance and trust, hoping that what he is going through will ultimately bring a greater good. He lives in hope.

What one of us hasn't been through the agony in the garden with Jesus? Single parents experience the passion of Jesus over and over as they carry the load of two parents on the back of one. Widowed, separated, or divorced people can recount a similar pain they have experienced as they walk in grief, sometimes all alone.

Children, too, experience the agony in the garden. The lives of many include some form of abuse, and they live in fear of what tonight or tomorrow might bring. Elderly persons, abandoned by family through death or desertion, know the agony of loneliness and fear. Married couples experience the pain of hurt and sadness as they struggle to make sure their relationship not only survives but remains healthy.

All of us, old or young, single or married, woman or man, poor or rich, lay person or clergy, nonChristian or Christian, know the reality of the thoughts and feelings of Jesus the night before he died. At the Good Friday service we feel Jesus' feelings. In this service his humanity meets ours. Our tears mix with his. And together with him, we await the resurrection.

> *Christ stands at the heart of . . . the "family of God."*
>
> CCC, 542

_____~ઙ_____

If we sat around the fire with them, . . .

_____~ઙ_____

Most likely, the first collected stories about Jesus were about his last days and his death. Later, the rest of the gospel stories were added as a sort of introduction, a preamble to the main event—his death and resurrection.

Wanting to keep the story of Jesus alive, the early Church gradually collected eyewitness accounts. People back then were very good at remembering. They nourished, educated, and entertained one another through the telling of stories. And, naturally, Christian people told the Jesus stories.

If we sat around the fire with them, we would probably overhear them saying such things as, "Remember the time when he was asleep in the boat and the storm . . ." or "Oh, here's a better one! The time when this boy had only two fish and five loaves of . . ." or "Hey, I was there when this family was bringing their daughter out to bury her, and Jesus came along and . . ." Maybe they did something that a family does at a wake. Tell the stories of Uncle This or Grandma That.

Almost every Christian probably knew the oft-repeated stories of Jesus' last days and his death and his resurrection. Perhaps the early believers told these stories on special days when they gathered to give thanks for his life among them. On these feast days, they remembered "that on the day before he died, he took . . ."

The arrival of the kingdom of God

A new logic arrives with the kingdom.

More than likely, the early eyewitnesses to Jesus' life probably forgot much of what he said and did. Yet they were sure to remember the really important things, especially if Jesus kept coming back to a particular topic time after time. The coming or the arrival of the kingdom of God was one of those often-repeated topics.

At the time of Jesus, the Jewish people based their religious hope on the creation of a time similar to their days of glory when David made them a mighty nation. So when Jesus spoke of a kingdom, his listeners thought something like the kingdom of David was coming again!

Also, the contemporaries of Jesus expected something to happen in their lifetime. Exactly what was expected depended on who was talking and to which group they belonged. Some thought that God would arrive armed with the full power of nature—lightning and thunder crashing everywhere and a couple of earthquakes thrown in for emphasis! In other words, the kingdom of God would begin in a rather dramatic fashion.

Others thought of God coming with a great army that would wipe out the Roman legions who occupied the land and bring political freedom to the Jews. Some looked forward to a fierce battle between the Sons of Light and the Sons of Darkness. During the time in which Jesus lived and died in Palestine, many people were predicting and expecting rather important events.

So when Jesus announced that the kingdom of God was at hand, some of his listeners probably looked up to the sky. Others might have looked out across the desert to see if the chariots were visible yet. Of course, we now know that Jesus was referring to a new kind of kingdom, a peace-filled kingdom. The sign of this kingdom would be the love shared by its inhabitants. Those who lived in the kingdom of God would not destroy their enemies, but love them. This was not exactly what was on the mind of many of his listeners.

To describe what life in his kingdom was like, Jesus turned to a popular form of explanation of his time called the parable. However, because the meaning behind these parables often defied conventional ways of thinking, they probably went right over the heads of many of his listeners whose hearts were not ready to receive the good news of God's unconditional love!

The parable of the owner of the vineyard, who went out at various times of the day to hire workers for harvesting his grapes, is a good example of a parable that confounded some and gave hope to others. In this parable, some laborers worked the whole day under the heat of the sweltering sun; others leisurely picked only a few bunches in the coolness at the end of the day. When the time came to pay the workers for their effort, the owner gave each the same amount.

"What's going on here?" complained the workers who had put in a solid eight hours. "We've been taken for a ride. This employer deserves to be reported to the Unfair Employment Practices Commission in Jerusalem. Who knows a good lawyer?"

The parables invite us into new ways of thinking about reality. For instance, in the kingdom none of us will care who gets more or less because each of us will have all we need or even desire. Those who enter the kingdom will be freed from anything that erodes the life of love. People will have a new set of priorities.

To those who have not chosen the kingdom, the behavior of Jesus' followers may appear foolhardy or even ridiculous. Imagine a shepherd who once owned one hundred sheep and when he lost just one of them, left the ninety-nine in search of the lost sheep.

Someone not in tune with Jesus' way of thinking might say, "Well, to my way of thinking, ninety-nine in the hand is worth more than one in the bush. Let's look at the real costs of this operation and make some prudent decisions. How much is the market value of ninety-nine sheep? How much for one sheep? Add up the figures. The decision is obvious!"

Not so, in the kingdom of God! We cannot reduce the value of something, even one sheep or especially one person, to dollars and cents. Never.

We can understand the teachings of Jesus only from within a kingdom perspective. It's much like when there is a sick child in a family. If we have eight children and one gets sick, we don't give just one-eighth of our attention to the sick one. A new logic arrives with the coming of the kingdom.

With the kingdom at hand, new experiences of life, new ways of relating, new ways of thinking and clusters of values unfolded. People entered this new realm through what we call conversion. Literally, this indicates a change of heart.

We need to spin around! Change our heart! Open ourselves to God. We want to allow the deep love of this God to touch our life, our very self. We want, deeply and mysteriously, to live as a new person.

Signs of the kingdom

The deep love of God and neighbor join.

The goodness and power of God is expressed particularly in what are called miracles. But the miracles of Jesus are not done to convince skeptics that Jesus is God or to prove that the message of Jesus is true. Miracles are signs of the presence of the kingdom. The blind see and the lame walk.

The dead are brought back to life. As long as we share our food, there is enough for everyone. Justice abounds.

The whole point of the kingdom is to introduce a wondrous new reality into the world. However, this wondrous reality is not without its own sadness and suffering. In fact, when the deep love of God and love of neighbor join together, sadness and suffering can be overwhelming. And this is exactly what happens as Jesus approaches the final days in Jerusalem.

The passion and death

Jesus died because of his great love for us and because of the horror of evil. He explicitly said that great love is shown when one gives up one's life for a friend. And for us, his friends, he did exactly that!

He shook the system, and we know that some perceived him as being at odds with the religious authorities of the day.

Why did Jesus die? One reason simply is that he was human. Humans die. But why did he have to die the horrible death of the cross? This is not easy to answer. We know that so much of what he taught caused problems for those in charge. He undermined those who used their power over people instead of in the service of people. He shook the system. And we know that some perceived him as being at odds with the religious authorities of the day. He disturbed their complacency.

We can name all kinds of possible explanations for why he was put to death, but in the end we are faced with yet another mystery of love. Quite simply, his love for us knew no limits. By dying the way he did, Jesus proved the depth of his love.

And the kind of love that was in Jesus is present all around us if we really notice. How many parents, married people, friends know both in theory and practice what giving all for the sake of somebody else entails? They have poured out their love seventy times seven already and are open to doing it over and over again. In many different ways we die for each other. This does not diminish in any way what Jesus did, but we need to remember that we have learned to love in his way.

During the Eucharist, the celebrant says, "This is my body which is given up for you." He is referring, of course, to the body of Jesus given for us in his passion and death so we might have life beyond this life. But what about the mom who works herself to the bone or the dad who is worried sick about his little family in the story at the beginning of this chapter? Are they not also giving up their bodies for the sake of others? Are they not living proof of the kingdom—here—now?

In this garden the night before he died on the cross, Jesus bathed in his own sweat and was torn apart inside and out. He was afraid. He was wishing things could be different. But in the end, he recited a line from a psalm in the Old Testament, a line that he'd probably said so many times before, "Into your hands . . . " Father. Abba. Daddy.

Doing this must not have been easy for Jesus, but most things that are truly worthwhile and good here on earth aren't easy. They're just worth it.

The reality of Jesus' pain is present in our own story.

Recalling the pain of another, especially the pain of someone we love, like Jesus, is never easy. Listening to the passion and imagining the horror of it is not easy either. When we hear the story of Jesus' agony in the garden and his death, some of own story wells up inside of us. So let us pause here and be present to the reality of Jesus' pain in our own story.

Let's take a deep breath and imagine early spring. Let's listen for the wonderful symphony of the universe: the birds, the breeze ruffling the tender leaves on the trees, the sound of water trickling somewhere in the distance. We feel that the garden is unusually warm for this time of year.

Like the father in our story, we sometimes know agony; it sits around our very being. Let us bring forth the worst of these memories and pay attention to it . . . just for the moment.

One of the greatest gifts we give one another as human beings is the sharing of our pain. When another responds, "I know what you mean. I've been there too," we establish a special bond between us. Jesus, too, knows what we mean. Jesus, truly human, truly one of us, has been "there" too.

Let us be here a moment with ourselves and with our God. Let us rest awhile in God's love. Let us entrust our agony to God. Let us trust that the spirit of Jesus, who is our friend, is within us.

A Psalm

Keep me safe from the trap that has been set for me;
shelter me from danger.
I place myself in your care.
You will save me, Lord;
you are a faithful God.
You hate those who worship false gods,
but I trust in you.

Psalm 31:4–6

In Family Pain

It's so hard, dear Lord,
for us to sometimes say,
"Into your hands . . ."
Because you see,
We really don't want to let go
Of whoever or whatever
We are in terrible fear of losing.
So help us now to
Say "Yes" and put ourselves,
Our very selves,
In that space and place
Of Jesus.
To say "Yes," when we hurt so much,
When a child is ill,
Or a teen is rebelling,
Or a love is dying,
Or a friend is going,
Or a parent is forgetting, still more.
And especially help us, dear Lord,
When our faith is weak
And we want to scream
NO!
For we know you're there, O God,
And all we need do is step through
That door or garden gate,
Like Jesus,
And you will never, ever go away. Amen.

CHAPTER EIGHT

Christ's Resurrection and the New Creation

"Dad! . . . This is your home too."

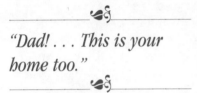

"It rents for $100 a week," the woman said. "No pets. No strange characters. This is a good place. You want it?"

The older gentleman glanced around. "Yes. It'll be fine." He handed her the money. "I'll go get my things and be back in an hour," he said.

Back out on the street he was glad for the air. He quickly got in his car and headed for his son's house.

"Dad! You're wrong! We want you here! This is your home too! The kids would be just sick if you left. Just because you're giving us the house doesn't mean you have to get out!" his oldest son yelled at him.

"I know that. You just don't understand. I'm old. I need a quiet little place just for me. It has nothing to do with you. It's about me and my needs. I'll come over a lot. The kids, and you and Debbie can come and see me. I'm just a few blocks away. It'll be good for me . . . and for you. And if it doesn't work out . . . I promise I'll let you know and be back. Now help me get this stuff into the car," the father ordered.

It was morning of the first day. He usually heard birds, so when he first woke, he was a bit confused. Then he remembered that he'd moved.

Suddenly he was aware of a gentle, rhythmic rocking in the room next door. Back and forth, back and forth. It reminded him of when Mother used to rock the babies. Funny how sounds remind you of things.

They both came out of their rooms at the same time, turned toward each other . . . and froze.

"Joe? What are you doing here?" the old woman asked in great surprise.

"Georgia! I didn't know you lived here! Well, I'll be darned. All those times we've played bingo you never mentioned where you lived! I just came . . . yesterday. And right now I can't think of a better place to be! I never imagined we'd be neighbors! Now you can get a ride to the parish with me instead of taking the bus!" The two smiled broadly at each other and walked down the hall.

With a flourish he opened the car door for his friend, and the two set off for church. On the way, he remembered how he had made his decision to move out and decided to share the memory with her.

"You know, it's a funny thing, but just last week, at church, I slipped in to make a visit to the Blessed Sacrament," he said, "and I actually sat there and told God all my frustrations at just being old. As if God had nothing better to do but hear me complain. And suddenly . . . Zap! The idea came to me!"

She smiled, encouraging him to go on. "Yes," the man said, "The idea just came . . . 'You're not dead yet!' I said. There's still life in this old body. Move out while you're still young enough!"

His friend suddenly looked strange. He drove on for about a minute, waiting for her to voice her thoughts. Finally, she said, "Joe, this is going to be hard to believe, but just last week I talked to God too. I told God I was so tired of taking the bus alone. I told God I couldn't do it anymore."

All age disappeared in the eyes of the two old people in the car. Wisdom and grace spoke gently to them. He reached over and touched her beautiful hand.

On that same day two of Jesus' followers were going
to a village named Emmaus, about seven miles from
Jerusalem, and they were talking to each other about
all the things that had happened. As they talked and
discussed, Jesus himself drew near and walked along
with them; they saw him but somehow did not
recognize him.

Luke 24:13–16

_____
*Jesus was a part of
bringing them together.*
_____

Do you suppose the two
people who met Jesus
along the road were a
couple? Or two women?
Perhaps a mother and
daughter or a mother
and son? Or, perchance, could they have been an
elderly couple on their way to play bingo (or whatever
else they did in those days!)?

It could have been anyone because Jesus' believers
were all ages and genders—whole families, members of
families, friends, people who started out as enemies.
They represented a cross section of people from that
time, and most likely, also people from our time. "They"
were us.

How fitting that the lonely persons in our opening
story, both struggling with the realities in their separate
lives, would find each other and that the finding
happened through a connection with their faith—
a community event in their local parish. And that they
would find each other as a result of prayer.

Jesus was a part of bringing them together and
bringing new life into their aging bodies! For he it is

who joins us as we walk our life; he meets us where we are, where we live so to speak. And he encourages and challenges us to walk with him.

Just as the young people today greet one another by saying, "Hey! What's up?" So Jesus wants to know, "What's up? What's doing?" Let's be honest with him for he can handle our honesty. Are we willing to accept his invitation to walk with him? He's here, right in the middle of our lives, with all its messiness and order, in the happy and the sad, in the bedlam before supper and in the search for a lost puppy. Jesus is here. We just don't always recognize him.

Yet at the same time this authentic, real body [of the risen Christ] possesses new properties of a glorious body; not limited by space and time but able to be present how and when he wills.

CCC, 645

All of us waved palm branches and shouted his name.

Let's imagine ourselves in Jerusalem a few days after the death of Jesus. We are one of his followers, and we join with other followers to grieve. We can't believe what has happened. Only a few days before, so many people greeted him enthusiastically as he rode into Jerusalem. So many people supported him. All of us waved palm branches and shouted his name. We were glad to know him; we were jubilant that he knew us. Now, he's dead.

All of us, all his followers, are depressed. We had hoped for so much, dreamed such big dreams. Now these dreams, tied up as they were to his teaching, no longer seem possible. Life was good for a while, but the dream is over. We remind ourselves not to get so enthusiastic the next time. We've learned a bitter lesson.

On our way to eat at a local cafe, we see one of those called the Twelve. His name is Matthew. We don't know whether to approach him. What can we say? Does he want to be alone in his grief? But we have a burning desire to know what happened to the old group. Have they just dispersed? Have any been jailed?

As we get closer to each other, we notice a large grin begin to spread across Matthew's bearded face when he recognizes us. Suddenly he runs to us and envelopes us in a huge embrace. For a minute, we lose our senses. What's happening? What's goin' on?

"My friends, did you hear? He's alive! He's here! He rose from the dead! Can you believe it?"

We're stunned, paralyzed. Could this be true? Can we risk believing again? Can we allow ourselves to be hopeful—again?

For centuries to come, until the present time, thoughtful people—women and men—ask the same question.

Easter people

The resurrection runs through our whole life.

Does the resurrection of Jesus make any real difference in our life? Is it important for us that Jesus came back from the dead? Is Easter an important day on our family calendar? On our spiritual calendar?

Many Catholics are taught that the resurrection is, indeed, a very important day because it was the day on which Jesus *fully* learned that he had been right to trust in God's love. The day, the event, was God's official seal of approval that what Jesus stood for, what he taught, what he did came from God. All that Jesus had proclaimed about God was true.

Another incredibly important aspect of the first Easter is that Jesus in his humanity became a new creation. Saint Paul speaks of the resurrection as the eighth day of creation. The work of God's spirit was far from over after the first seven days. God's work was only beginning.

One way to think of this would be to consider our building a bridge halfway over a deep canyon. Of what value would such a bridge be if it did not span the valley below and take us to the other side? And so, once the eighth day came to be, the bridge arched above the valley, touched the other side and set us in a new place. A new day dawned over the mountains on both sides of the bridge and over the dark valley below.

On the day God raised Jesus from death, we became a new creation. We are now Easter people, living with a new spirit, one of hope and confidence. Now the hunger described in the first chapter of this book is satisfied in some real measure. In fact, if we open ourselves to God's love as revealed in Jesus, we discover that the resurrection runs through the happenings of our whole life.

When we Christians gather for Eucharist, we give thanks for life, not death; we celebrate life, not death. From Jesus' resurrection, we draw hope. (Easter people live with hope.) Jesus' resurrection allows us to face the big and little deaths in our own life with hope.

This hope is not the same as optimism. Optimism is looking at the brighter of two sides. For instance, we look at the four ounces in the eight-ounce glass and proclaim it is half full. We look at the bright side. Our optimism is based on evidence.

Hope, on the other hand, looks death straight in the eye, and says, "There will be life." Hope is the Christian virtue of "in spite of." Hope sees and acknowledges evil, sin, destruction, and human failings all around and still believes. Together we say, "I believe in the resurrection of the dead! And therefore I believe in all kinds of big and little resurrections!"

The Easter stories

One of the moves Jesus could have made that first Easter day was to knock on the door of Pilate, the man who ordered his

Jesus revealed himself to those who already believed.

death, and say, "Remember me?" What a headline the *Jerusalem Times* would have run the next day!

But that's not what happened. The resurrection appearances are very selective. Jesus revealed himself to those who already believed. He wanted to show them that he was still around, especially when they gathered in his name. In a way, he was fulfilling something he had said a couple of years before. He had promised, "Where two or three come together in my name, I am there with them." Now Jesus wanted all those who believed to know that he meant what he said!

In this Church, newly created in the death and resurrection of Jesus, he was, would be, present to those who believed. Yet this presence differed from those days when he had walked the dusty lanes of Galilee. His body was different. We know this because his intimate friends didn't always recognize him. Still, he truly had a body as Thomas, who put his finger in the wounds, found out. Yet, in his risen body, Jesus came and went as he willed.

Even after he officially left his followers through what we call his ascension into heaven, the Church realized that Jesus was still with them and, in fact, was now within them. They began to notice that they were able to do the things he had done before his death. There was (and is) a real presence of Jesus in the people of the Church! Especially when we love and serve others.

Let's look at the people Jesus singled out for special appearances. He comes first to Mary Magdalene, a close friend, and tells her to tell the rest of his followers. (In the gospels of Matthew, Mark, and Luke, Mary Magdalene is with other women; in John's gospel, she is alone in the garden. What is consistent in the various accounts is that women take the lead in being the first witnesses to the resurrection.) He also appears to his disciples while they are hiding in fear.

In another appearance, Jesus meets two disciples on a walk about seven miles outside Jerusalem. When he joins them on their walk, they do not recognize him! They engage in a discussion over the events of the last two days. Then they stop to eat. Jesus "breaks bread" with them and then leaves. Upon his departure, they realize that the traveler was Jesus and they remember that their hearts burned within them when he spoke to them on their journey and opened the Scriptures to them. (See Luke 24:32.)

And finally, we can read about an early morning scene on the side of the lake. The apostles have apparently returned to their earlier profession and are out fishing again. Their luck is down and Jesus calls out to them from the shore to cast their nets on the other side of the boat.

The apostles do not immediately recognize Jesus. Nevertheless, they take his advice. The result? They can hardly manage all they catch! It is then that they recognize him, and Peter, overcome with emotion, jumps into the water to rush to him. While the rest are attending to their haul, Jesus prepares a fire for a barbecue breakfast for them on the beach. They come ashore and feast on fish and bread. The banquet began!

The new creation

While the old creation may look a lot like the new creation, we can find some very important differences. The risen Christ is now the focal point of the new creation. His presence brings us hope and alerts us to the opportunity of encountering the spirit of Jesus at any moment of our lives.

Who's to say Jesus is not part of almost everything that speaks of care and concern, of people changing their lives?

We may meet him in another person—in a family member, a stranger, a friend, even in ourselves. This new presence of Jesus is what the Church will later call the Mystical Body of Christ.

In our little opening story, we read an endearing account of two lonely, elderly people. An ordinary kind of event, which could happen to a lot of people. But this encounter is special in its own way. Two acquaintances on their way to becoming close friends. Two people living alone, no longer feeling alone.

But, we Christians ask, is that all that is happening? No. What we witness in this simple story is two people pledging a gesture of mutual kindness—serving each other. In their own minds, the other is the answer to a prayer.

Let us seek to recognize Jesus in this scene. Who's to say that he's not part of almost everything that speaks of care and concern, of love and understanding, of people changing their lives for the better. In a new day, anything wonderful can happen.

The risen Christ lives in the hearts of his faithful while they await that fulfillment [our future resurrection]. In Christ, Christians "have tasted . . . the powers of the age to come" (Hebrews 6:5) and their lives were swept up by Christ. . . .

CCC, 655

Jesus now lives in our homes and families.

The Church invites us and challenges us to put the risen Christ right in the center of our thinking about creation and everything else! Now, everything is different. When one of the members of a family changes radically, the change affects the whole system. The whole system is something new. By his resurrection, the Lord Jesus was recognized as the center of creation, the center of the entire universe! He became over and above, because and instead of . . . everything! He created all anew. And his resurrection affected all the members of God's family.

We have traveled the full course with Jesus: His divine beginning. His coming to us in a very human way—a normal pregnancy and birth with a non-traditional foster family. His becoming flesh and dwelling among us as one of us.

Then the experience of his life—the happiness and the pain of Jesus that led to a hill on which he was crucified. And then, on a bright sunny morning, the stone is pushed back, and Jesus Christ, having been raised from the dead, takes a stroll in the fresh air of the universe and says, "It is all new."

The remainder of the story unfolds as the rest of us react to this new world. A world filled with the essence, the presence of God. Does all this make any difference to us? Do we open to his invitation to life with deep hope and a strong confidence that deep down, the universe—our life—has all been recreated? Have we accepted this invitation to live a new life?

Jesus now lives in our homes and within our families. He lives in the spaces between us, like the couple in our opening story. He dwells with us and between us. Ever present. Wherever two or three are gathered . . . there, too, is Jesus.

A Psalm

I praise the Lord, because he guides me,
and in the night my conscience warns me.
I am always aware of the Lord's presence;
he is near, and nothing can shake me.
And so I am thankful and glad,
and I feel completely secure,
because you protect me from the power of death.
I have served you faithfully,
and you will not abandon me to the world of the dead.
You will show me the path that leads to life;
your presence fills me with joy
and brings me pleasure forever.

Psalm 16:7–11

A Psalm of Walking toward Life

aths are made by human feet.
Paths are made by the journey
And not prepaved.

With each step another decision:
This way or that?
Where will I find the life
I so much want?

Blessed am I and blessed are all of us;
We never, ever walk alone.
You, Lord Jesus, whisper the best direction
To my distracted heart.
Sometimes I hear well;
Sometimes I'm not sure.

A favor I ask of you, O Lord,
If I seem to stray from the path of life,
The life of fullness you always offer,
Speak a little louder.
Amen.

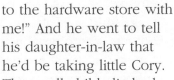

CHAPTER NINE
The Coming of the Holy Spirit

He reached forward and put his hand in hers.

"Hop in!" Grandpa said. "Of course you can go to the hardware store with me!" And he went to tell his daughter-in-law that he'd be taking little Cory. The small child climbed onto the front seat of his grandpa's car. Spotting the jelly beans on the seat he helped himself. "Grandpa always buys these," he thought to himself as he struggled with his seat belt. "I'm gonna ask him to buy me something."

The ride wasn't long. When the two got to the store, it was crowded with Saturday shoppers, and they couldn't find a shopping cart. So the big guy held the little guy's hand, a human ritual of great significance.

"Grandpa, can I have some candy? Huh? Can I? Can I, Grandpa, huh?"

"Nope. Too close to lunch," the older man echoed his own mother's words. "Those jelly beans in the car were enough."

"But, Grandpa, Mommy always lets me eat something at the store. Don't they have candy here? Huh, Grandpa? Don't they? Huh, Grandpa?"

When the grandfather found the screw bin, he had to let go of Cory's hand because he needed to count out the screws and put them in a bag.

The little boy saw the red shopping cart go by with the little dog in it, and his instinct said "Follow that puppy!" The lady was walking fast, but he watched the puppy until the woman paid at the check-out line and left the store. Then he turned around to ask his grandpa if he didn't think that he should have a puppy. But Grandpa wasn't there! He wasn't anywhere!

Cory's body filled with fear. He ran forward to the cross aisle and quickly glanced in both directions. "Grandpa! Grandpa!" he called.

People looked at him in quick glances, but he didn't see them. Where was his grandpa? Suddenly, Cory began to run down the aisles, yelling, "Grandpa! Grandpa, where are you? Grandpa!"

Tears streamed down his face as he yelled at the top of his lungs, "Grandpa left me! He went home for lunch! Grandpa? Where are you?" He threw himself to the floor and wailed, "Mommy! Daddy! Mommy! Where's my mommy?"

A lady he didn't know hunched down next to him and said something. He couldn't hear what she said because of his sobs. Then she lifted him from the floor and stood him on his feet. He was still scared, but when she put her hand out to him, he reached forward and put his hand in hers.

> *The One whom the Father has sent into our hearts, the Spirit of his Son, is truly God.*
>
> CCC, 689

At that time the disciples came to Jesus, asking, "Who is the greatest in the Kingdom of heaven?"

So Jesus called a child to come and stand in front of them, and said "I assure you that unless you change and become like children, you will never enter the Kingdom of heaven. The greatest in the Kingdom of heaven is the one who humbles himself and becomes like this child.

"See that you don't despise any of these little ones. Their angels in heaven, I tell you, are always in the presence of my Father in heaven.

In just the same way your Father in heaven does not want any of these little ones to be lost."

Matthew 18:1–5, 10, 14

The kingdom is for everyone.

Sometimes in the gospel stories Jesus brings in a child to teach the grown-ups. Why? To underscore the importance of our becoming like children in order to be open to the kingdom; to teach us that the kingdom is for everyone—young and not-so-young alike; and to stress that children are valuable and vulnerable members of the kingdom.

We all understand the vulnerability of a child. We're family people. We either have children or have taken care of them.

Jesus' greatest concern is that not one of us, child or grown-up, be lost to the kingdom. Who of us has never been lost? Perhaps while driving to someplace new. Or while rushing to an appointment in a huge office building. Or when shopping in a sprawling mall.

Or in a store, like the child in the story. Being lost is an awful feeling. No matter how old we are, we know a moment or two of raw fear, however fleeting.

Jesus worried about that. Not so much that we'd get lost in traffic or in the mall or in an office building, but that one of us would somehow wander off and he'd lose us. Think of that . . . he'd lose us! His love for us is so strong that he lived with the fear something would happen to us. Much like that grandfather in the story must have felt or how any adult who loves a child would feel. The fear of losing him or her.

So, part of God's great plan is not to abandon us (even in a store). We are never alone. For the Spirit is always with us. All we need do is take the hand when it is offered. All we need do is trust.

Jesus heals the sick and blesses little children by laying hands on them. . . . The Church has kept this sign of the . . . outpouring of the Holy Spirit.

CCC, 699

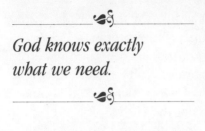

*God knows exactly
what we need.*

The pain of loss is among the most difficult experiences any of us face in our life, especially when loss happens in our family. Most of us have felt this pain, and depending on who or what has been lost, our feeling does not easily go away. Nor should it, because a piece of our life and our heart is no longer present to us in the same way. Jesus himself expressed deep sorrow and sadness at the news of the death of his friend Lazarus.

The first followers of Jesus felt the pain of his departure. These staunch disciples, Jesus' closest friends, went into hiding. They were afraid! Even after they knew the reality of the resurrection, they were fearful. In the story of the first Pentecost, we find them locked in a room, filled with trepidation, because they were facing danger. This is not an especially good way to start a movement that would change the world.

But that's okay. We human beings always need time to adjust to new situations. And these women and men were truly in a new situation. They didn't know quite what to do next. They needed a jump start, so to speak. They needed something or someone to get them moving again. And that's exactly what God planned. Our God knows exactly what we need.

Suddenly there was a stirring in the locked room. The assembled group felt that something was about to happen. The Scriptures tell us that all at once tongues of fire appeared and then broke apart and hovered above each of the people gathered in the room. Without burning them, in the sense we know, this fire immediately did something within them. Their fears fell away, like leaves from a tree in the fall. Courage and enthusiasm filled them.

What happened? Each was filled with the Holy Spirit, God's Spirit, the Spirit of Christ. Within them, the Spirit came to dwell for the long journey ahead. The image of fire as used in the Scriptures refers to God's energizing presence. It's sort of a "Don't just sit there . . . do something." That's pretty much what the Holy Spirit did on Pentecost and continues to do within and for us today. "Get up! Enter into your life. I have plans for you!"

What followed on that Pentecost day was amazing. Once almost afraid to go near a window, the disciples now threw open the doors and ran out into the street. A crowd was outside, for Jerusalem was always busy and nosy with travelers from far distant places. Without any hesitation, the followers of Jesus began to tell everyone about him; they invited their listeners to join them in following the Messiah, the one they had all been waiting for.

And we who come from different lands and perhaps speak a different language note that when the disciples spoke, each person heard them in his or her own language! With God all things are possible. In this instance, immediate communication was needed and happened! Once again the Scriptures assure us that God is the God of everyone.

The Spirit as advocate and consoler

When life is difficult and hurtful, God is on our side.

Over the kitchen table, we have been discussing so many wonderful parts of our Catholic faith. Sometimes we talk about our relationships with those closest to us, especially our family. We also talk about good communication, honesty, and openness, and about our being on a long journey of faith. We make this walk with others.

Sometimes we rely on others and others depend on us. Sometimes we need to be in control of our life. Sometimes we need to let go and let God be God for us.

In all of this, we have noticed how our God will not leave us alone. God will never abandon us. At the Last Supper, Jesus had been clear: God would not leave us orphaned. This is the heart of our belief in the Holy Spirit.

In what is called the history of salvation, we learn how God has been working with us and loving us all along the way. To help us understand something about the importance of diversity within God, the Scriptures sometimes divide God's work between the three Persons of God.

Thus, our Catholic tradition often attributes the creative work of God to the First Person of the Blessed Trinity—the Creator; the redemptive (saving us for God) work of God to the Second Person of the Blessed Trinity—the Redeemer; and the sanctifying (our being made holier) work of God to the Third Person—the Sanctifier, or Holy Spirit.

(This way of speaking of God's work may confuse us. But God does not "switch" persons. God is always fully present in all God's activity. There is only one God. When we speak of "the indwelling of the Holy Spirit," we really mean God—not a part of God, not something made by God, or sent from God, but God.)

Scripture describes the Holy Spirit as an advocate—someone who speaks on behalf of someone else. This is another indicator of our special connectedness with God. How wonderful to know this presence is here all the time. How consoling, when life is difficult and hurtful, to know that God is on our side.

The early Christians believed that the Spirit of God was with them. The Spirit played a conscious role in their life, especially in hard times. During the first three centuries of the Christian era, the Church experienced a terribly difficult time. The political powers did not want this movement of Jesus' followers to continue. Christianity was too radical, too threatening.

However, these troubles did not mean God had abandoned those who were working so hard to bring Jesus' message to the world. God was with the early Christians as they strove to overcome evil and to preach the message of God's relentless love. The Spirit was with the early Christians as one who consoles and comforts when they grew weary.

Sometimes we blame God too easily for almost every imaginable misfortune. We seem to feel that if God really loved us, we would never have a headache, an unbalanced checkbook, or a cranky parent. But the Spirit of God is with us. In the long run, God never abandons us. God helps us journey to the fullness of who we are called to be.

The gifts of the Spirit

Wonderful qualities, especially designed for living in family.

The early Christians were not cookie-cutter versions of one another. They were not zombies either. Clearly, among them were the usual variety of personalities, families, and cultural backgrounds. But that was to be expected. But each Christian possessed special gifts, personal qualities, or talents needed by the community. Scripture says, "Many gifts but one Spirit."

Some believers left Jerusalem and spread the Gospel to distant lands. Some established and organized communities. Some of Jesus' followers were gifted in explaining the Gospel to others. They were teachers. Some were gifted in understanding the spiritual depth of people; some offered good advice. Some helped others in discernment, a process in prayer for identifying the will of God in a particular situation. Some had the talent to lead prayer. Some were excellent in helping the sick, the needy, the poor.

The early Christians felt led by the Spirit to these activities, and they believed that they were gifted by God's Spirit for their particular task. And what's more, the gifts seemed to be evenly scattered throughout the communities, so that all the needs of the community were provided for through various gifted persons. What was also apparent was that all persons had gifts. Some gifts were more obvious than others, but the Spirit gave gifts to all the followers of Jesus. This is the foundation of what later was called a vocation, a calling by God's Spirit to serve others and to serve God in a special way.

The presence of the Spirit within people also created results in their personal lives. In one of the many letters we find in the New Testament, we have a wonderful listing of these fruits of the Spirit: love, joy, peace, patience, kindness, goodness, faithfulness, humility, and self-control. (Galatians 5:22–23)

These are certainly wonderful qualities no matter where one is, but they seem especially designed for living in community with others—for living in family. What's important for us to note is that these fruits are all about happiness; they are qualities of a happy person.

Of what significance is this? Simply that as Christians we are not to be glum, overly serious, or weighed down by the troubles of the world. A genuine smile joined with a gesture of kindness is a clear sign of the Spirit's presence in ordinary life. This is what we call ordinary holiness.

However, when this smile and this kindness occur, we are far from being ordinary. Every time we see someone reaching out to others with one of the gifts, or fruits, of the Holy Spirit, we see another Pentecost, another coming of the Spirit among us!

Family members of God's household

God's "blood" flows through our veins.

The presence of the Spirit changes us, transforms us, make us a member of God's family. In the letter to the Ephesians, the letter writer describes us as "members of the household of God." (Ephesians 2:19) In a sense, God's "blood" flows through our veins; God's thoughts (when our thoughts are good and of love) flow through our mind. We are not describing fantasy here, but reality. Members of the early Church were realistic when describing God. They described what they experienced and what they believed. They felt the Spirit. And most often, they felt the Spirit as members of a family, including the family of God. And the two were one.

Since that day [Pentecost], the Kingdom announced by Christ has been open . . . in the humility of flesh and in faith.

CCC, 732

The Spirit is pure gift.

The little child in our opening story gives us an example of wonderful openness: Grandpa will buy me something; puppies are for holding and petting; you have to trust that ladies will take you to your grandpa.

Such innocence. Such precious trust. However, what one of us, when reading that story, didn't worry that the woman would kidnap Cory and take him not to his grandfather but to her car? Daily we read of children being abducted by adults and even by other children. Evil has crawled into every aspect of our lives. However, God still invites and challenges us to open ourselves to the Spirit who is always present to us. This Spirit is pure gift.

And with this gift comes still more. Each of us has been given gifts that make God obvious to the world. Which aspects of ourselves are appreciated and needed by others, by the world? Our musical talent? Our ability to listen well? The great joy we take in children? Our empathy with teenagers? Our aptitude for organizing and planning? Our green thumb? Our facility as speakers? Or writers? Or teachers? Our ability to make others laugh? Our love of animals? Our aptitude for technical things? Our enthusiasm on the playing field? What are our gifts?

Are we using them? If we are, we know a great peace and happiness whenever we use our gifts. That's God's idea. That's the Spirit acting within us.

To get in touch with the reality of the Holy Spirit acting within us, we might ask someone we love to help us recognize our gifts. What do they see in us? What do they think we do best? What do we do that gives life to the world? Each of us is unique, special, one of a kind. Each of us has a particular collection of gifts. Each of us is holy. And that is a gift too.

A Psalm

Happy are those who have the God of Jacob to help them
and who depend on the Lord their God, / the Creator
of heaven, earth, and sea, / and all that is in them. /
He always keeps his promises; / he judges in favor
of the oppressed / and gives food to the hungry. / The
Lord sets prisoners free and gives sight to the blind. He
lifts those who have fallen; / he loves his righteous
people. / He protects the strangers who live in our
land; / he helps widows and orphans, / but takes the
wicked to their ruin. / The Lord is king forever. / Your
God, O Zion, will reign for all time. / Praise the Lord!

Psalm 146:5–10

Unwrapping Our Family

less us, O God,
For these, your gifts,
Which you have given to us,
Which we sometimes don't even recognize.

The time to sleep in on Saturday
Or a fistful of dandelions
Or even mud on our floor

Or another payday.

And bless us too, O Lord,
For the gifts of dishes to do
Or groceries to buy or cars to fix
Or diapers to change or jeans to wash
Or a phone that rings
Or (yet another) birthday to celebrate.

For in all of these,
All of these, and more,
We find the presence of you
Especially in the gift
Of each other.
Amen.

CHAPTER TEN
The Church Is God's People

*We're members.
Just like in a family.*

They spotted four chairs near the door. The littlest Sullivan ran to save them for the doughnut-bearing family. Somehow it didn't feel like Mass without this weekly coffee and doughnut ritual!

The Martins were right next to them, and the two families quickly exchanged their weekly hellos and began to talk! Of course, besides Little League, their favorite topic of conversation was the Parish Council—especially the big decisions about the school and religious education.

But Tom Martin was a bit quiet this Sunday, and so John asked his friend what was up. The answer was not expected.

"You know, John. I sat at Mass today, listening to Father's words, and thinking about all the money going out to pay off these people who've been molested by priests. And I just couldn't quit thinking about it! I still am, obviously! Can you believe it? And they say it's not coming out of our pockets. Baloney! What other pockets does the Church have?" the young father asked. Clearly, he was still upset.

"You know," Sally Sullivan joined in, "this abuse is happening all over the country. It's embarrassing. I can't believe we—they—have covered up all of this so much! No matter what! This is still our Church.

We, the people, are the victims and the ones who have to pay for the abuse! It's terrible."

"You bet it is!" Donna Martin interjected, "I wonder if the Church realizes how terrible? You know, everywhere I go when the subject of the Church comes up, somebody eventually gets around to talking about pedophiles or other sex-related topics about the Church. It sure does affect me! I'm almost embarrassed to say I'm Catholic!"

"I think it's really hurt the Church," John added. "I mean, there's enough evil happening in the world. Let alone in the Church!"

"But you know," the other young father said, "one of the amazing things is exactly the point that it affects all of us. Not only are the victims and their families terribly affected—the four of us and our kids are! I guess it reminds me of what happened in our family when we found out my sister's husband had been cheating on her for years . . . sleepin' round with just about everybody!" He took a sip of his coffee and bit into a doughnut while his wife and friends digested his story.

After chewing for a few seconds, the young father continued, "And my sister and the kids were so hurt. It was a real blow to the whole family, on both sides! Then the divorce and all. Sort of a crime against the family, ya' know what I mean? And everybody has suffered . . . and still are. Especially the kids. All kinds of victims."

"But you know," his wife added, "if you think about that even more, one of the reasons all of us as family were affected is because we belong to the family. What one person does affects all of us . . . good or bad! And it's the same with this pedophile stuff. We're all affected because we belong to this family! We're members. Just like in a family!"

The four young parents sat there quietly. A soft blanket of sadness gently rested on the table between them.

Christ is like a single body, which has many parts; it is still one body, even though it is made up of different parts. In the same way, all of us, whether Jews or Gentiles, whether slaves or free, have been baptized into the one body by the same Spirit, and we have all been given the one Spirit to drink.

So then, the eye cannot say to the hand, "I don't need you!" Nor can the head say to the feet, "Well, I don't need you!" If one part of the body suffers, all the other parts suffer with it; if one part is praised, all the other parts share its happiness.

1 Corinthians 12:12–13, 21, 26

A beautiful image of belonging to one another.

The words above are easy to relate to for two simple reasons: We all have a body, and we all belong to what we call other bodies, or systems. In other words, we ourselves are a collection of interconnected parts (knees, ears, heart), and we are a part of other, bigger systems (a school, a corporation, an apartment building, a town). We are part of the most basic system of life itself—a family.

And we all know what can happen in any body (system) when something happens to one of its members: All the other members are affected. When we hit our thumb with a hammer, our whole body hurts! It's the same in other systems. When one of the parts feels great or awful, the feeling is felt by all the rest of the body. (If the boss has a bad day, so do we all!)

So, in a beautiful image of belonging to one another, the writer of this letter in the New Testament tells us how interdependent we are. Each of us, through the

Holy Spirit, is a part of the whole. We need each other. When any part of the whole suffers, all of us suffer.

This is what is happening in our opening story. In this case, the belonging to something larger has to do with the body spoken of in the above passage—the broader Church. And, as we know, each family is also church—the domestic church, the church of the home.

So here our families sit, experiencing the rest of their Sunday morning Mass of coffee and doughnuts, which is something they do often. And, like any part of a whole, because of something else occurring in the body, namely abuse by the clergy, they are filled with feelings.

Perhaps the most important aspect of their interchange isn't the anger, because that just masks something else, usually another hurt. The most important aspect is that they feel!

If they didn't care, if they did not belong, in the sense of longing to be a part of the Church, they wouldn't be so affected. If they didn't love the broader Church, they could not be so hurt. The old saying "The only reason you can hurt me is because I love you" is true.

What a wonderful, and sometimes sad, expression of being connected. Sexual abuse by Catholic clergy (or any other Christian minister or leader) is something that affects all of us. And while our Church is doing a great deal to undo past wrongs and to change what needs to be changed in the present, for a healthier future, the abusive actions of the clergy still hurt the whole body. They hurt us.

In the meantime, our two families sit somewhere in Saint Anywhere parish, like thousands of others in homes and other gatherings around the world, and discuss what's happening in the family—our Catholic family.

God is present within a very human reality.

The Church is the gathering of those of us who have responded to God's Spirit. The Spirit invites us into a special relationship with Jesus. Jesus said that his followers would be recognized by the love they had for one another or by their care for those in need. They were to make real in themselves God's love for all. We are not perfect by a long shot; we fall and get back up. But, made new by the Spirit, we are always trying harder to love more fully.

The above description of the Church may cause us to shake our head in dismay. We see it as a great theory, but very, very hard to put into practice. Sometimes we look around in the Church as we know it, perhaps our local parish, and simply wonder what happened. What happened to the truth and beauty and generosity and the gifts of the early Church? Where did they go? Were they ever there in the first place?

When these questions plague us, we need to face a very important aspect of the Church. We, the Church, are both human and divine. God is present within a very human reality.

In studying the Church, we learn that throughout its history, the people of the Church were a mixture of the same kind of people we have in the world today. Even the first disciples of Jesus were known to get into frequent arguments with one another. They, too, had their good, and not so good, days.

The story at the beginning of this chapter expresses what being a part of the life of the Church means. While deep within us we desire to be a part of a perfect group, a dream team, we know that this isn't a realistic expectation.

In life, we are constantly faced with imperfection, misunderstanding, and outright evil more often than most of us would wish. We have to deal with our own imperfection and shortcomings. Which is to say that we all stand in need of God's forgiving and healing grace. And just as in a family, we stay.

The Church as the Body of Christ

The heart of faith knows it.

Paul described the Church as the Body of Christ. The apostle intended here a very realistic interpretation of the notion of body. He believed that the Church is the risen body of Christ. This risen body has a new way of being, a new form of existence here on earth. The Spirit of Jesus is present in the Church. That is, the Spirit is present in us, the members of the Church.

The life of this body is the life of Jesus. Thus, we are connected with Jesus. He is with us and we are with him. He is in us; we in him. Maybe our human eyes cannot see this connection, but the heart of faith knows it.

In the body of Jesus, we are connected also to each other. Today, we know that every cell in our body is in some way connected with every other cell. Tweak the toe and the eye blinks. When we think about climbing a mountain, our heart beats faster. If we are depressed, we might have an ache in our stomach. A great meal makes us feel better all over. It is as if there were millions of electrical wires in our body and the receivers are all connected in some way.

Our interpersonal life is this way too. We get a phone call from a friend who is depressed. We hang up and all of a sudden we feel down too. We receive a friendship card from our old college roommate from whom we have not heard in twenty years. We read the words "Your friend forever!" and a rush of warm feeling envelops our body. Everything in our body is connected.

So, with the Body of Christ Jesus, the Church, we are all connected, one to the other. Still, while we can easily see that our individual body is one, grasping that the Body of Jesus—the Church—is one is less obvious, but no less real.

Both one and many—at the same time

What holds the Church together? Some kind of celestial glue? Shared feelings? Again, the teachings of Paul are clear. Love is what holds us together. What really connects us is the affection, care, good will, and simple gestures of kindness and service that we give to one another. And this love comes from God's Spirit. Drawn together by the Spirit of God, the Church retains its identity as a body because love flows through its veins.

> *Love is what holds us together. What really connects us is the simple gestures of kindness and service that we give one another.*

This is partly why experiencing a lack of love within the Church is so sad, so devastating. When we encounter power or manipulation or basic distrust instead of love, we feel betrayed. In the long history of the Church we meet many examples of the Church experiencing division and the division turning into hostility. One side thinks itself right and judges the other side wrong. Often the opposing sides do little communicating, a sure sign that the life of love is not flowing very well between them.

Marks or signs of the Church

We are connected to the faith of the apostles in our holy work, in our holy play.

In the great tradition of our Church, four characteristics, or marks, are part of its life. The Church is said to be **one** in the sense of oneness in the Spirit. The one love who gave (and gives) the Church its life. Being one does not mean everyone or everything has to be the same.

The phrase "Unity does not require uniformity" is important for the life of the Church. Families struggle over issues of unity. We all wonder how much sameness of behavior and belief is required for our family to remain close and intact. Usually, in the presence of a good measure of real love, a family is comfortable letting go and accepting diversity in its members. But when a family cannot find altruistic or nonjudgmental love within itself, then that family demands a greater conformity. We must always remember that the Church is a family too.

The second mark of the Church is that it is **holy.** This means that its life comes from God and that its life is meant to bring the members of the Church—us—closer to God.

The third mark of the Church is that it is **catholic.** This is not meant to refer to one church—namely the Roman Catholic Church. *Catholic* means that deep down the Church is the same all over the world. It also means that the Church fits into any culture of the world and reflects that culture, those persons.

And the final mark is that the Church is **apostolic.** This has several very related meanings. First, *apostolic* means that the community of believers, the Church, can trace its existence back to the first apostles of Jesus and their teachings. These were the first witnesses of Jesus.

Because the apostles were close to Jesus (the source of the Church's life), their accounts of Jesus are the foundation of the Church. Thus, there needs to be a recognizable connection between any later teachings of the Church and the teaching of the earliest Church.

Finally, *apostolic* means that the members of the Church, those of us who came later, are connected to the faith of the apostles in our actions, in our holy work, in our holy play, and in our mission to bring Christ's life and love to the world.

Church structure and offices

The Church gradually evolved into a social structure that in some ways imitated the existing social structures of the place and time in which it took hold. For example, the first young churches—commu-

None of us are second-class citizens, third cousins once removed.

nities of believers in towns and cities throughout the Roman Empire—were very similar to families, especially extended families. They were even called "households of faith." The heads of those churches may even have been married couples or single people.

As the Church grew, especially in the larger cities, there developed the diocese. (At least that's what we call it today.) The person who provided leadership for these large church communities was called a bishop. Eventually, as the Church spread out over the known world, the diocese of Rome (where Peter and Paul were martyred) became the most important diocese and its leader (the bishop of Rome) was identified as "the first one among equals." Eventually he was called the pontiff, meaning "bridge builder," and later the pope. Years afterward, bishops in very large cities were called archbishops. Finally, some became cardinals, whose special role was to elect new popes.

The Church was called hierarchical because some roles in the organization of the Church were above others in power and authority. However, this never meant that one person in the Church was any closer to God, any holier, or any better than anyone else. Roles differed, but all were important—from the bottom to the top, so to speak. Notice how some of this reminds us of the positions and roles in the family. Actually, in the early Church, people could be made bishops only if they showed themselves to have the ability to care for a family and a household.

Early in the 1960s, the Church called an important council to renew its life and to bring it into the twentieth century. At this council, called Vatican II, the Church defined its own identity. It began its description by saying that the source of its life is God. God is present in and to the Church, and God is available to those who are part of the Church.

Then the council brought forward a concept used to describe the chosen people of God, the Jews. This rich, biblical phrase—the People of God—implies that each and every member of the Church is a full member. None of us are second-class citizens, auxiliary members, farm teams, third cousins once removed. No. All of us are just people, loved and cherished, challenged and graced to be what God intended in the first place.

We belong to each other, warts and beauty and all.

Sometimes we hear the words *the Church* meaning the BIG Church, the authority, and we react as we would to the words "The IRS called." A wave of anxiety, of avoidance, of guilt, of confusion, anger, hurt . . . or a hundred or so other human reactions run through us. Unfortunately, rarely do we have warm, comfortable feelings. The reasons are as numerous as we are.

Perhaps we feel emotionally attached because of our family's history in the parish, or perhaps we feel a sense of belonging because of all the people we've met there or perhaps we even feel something having to do with money. Either we think "they" spent too much on this or that, or "we" need a new parking lot! The structure in which we meet is also indeed called the church. Why? Because it is the place, the holy space, where we, the Church, gather together with other members of families who also believe.

All of us are the Church. And we know this in our hearts. That's why we get so angry or hurt sometimes. It's also why we sometimes cry tears of joy. We belong to each other. What another member does or is or feels or thinks affects all of us. God wants the Church to be that way. We belong to each other, warts and beauty and all.

Do we ever think of the Church as belonging to us? Do we long to be with the other members of the body? Do we reach out to others in our Catholic faith family and help them feel a part of the body, a part of us?

And if we do not feel a sense of belonging, do we ever think about why? And is there anything we can do to change that? Do we like coffee and doughnuts? Perhaps that's the place to start.

A Psalm

You prepare a banquet for me, / where all my enemies can see me; / you welcome me as an honored guest / and fill my cup to the brim. / I know that your goodness and love will be with me all my life; / and your house will be my home as long as I live.

Psalm 23:5–6

New Houses of Our God

These days, O God, where do you dwell?
Where is your place of residence?
Where can we gather to find you?

If we need you, where do we go?
"I dwell in a beautiful temple
That stretches to the heavens,
In a land rich in all ways,
In a countryside of immense beauty."

Dear God, knowing that you are in such a
    wonderful place,
Even more do we seek the way.
More excitedly our heart beats
Just thinking about being with you.

"And I want you to come as well;
Whenever we are apart, you are on my mind.
The path has been cleared,
The door is open—come."

And once more, Lord, where is your house?

"With you, my friends,
Wherever you are, I am there.
You are now my beautiful temple
That stretches to the heavens
In a land rich in all ways.
In a countryside of immense beauty."
Amen.

CHAPTER ELEVEN
The Family as Church of the Home

They found him in the stories they told of his loving them.

"Dad's dead," her brother said. She'd dreaded these words for months.

He'd been sick all this last year. But no matter how much she rehearsed hearing the words that announced his death, she wasn't prepared. They crashed into the center of her being.

First, calls to Mom and the other "kids." Then calls to her own children—"Grandpa died." Airline arrangements. The pull to go and not to go. "I don't want to go bury Dad! God, I don't want to do this!" her pain said.

"I'm going tomorrow," she told her oldest son, "and Erin is going with me so I'm not alone. The rest of you will come on Wednesday. We'll pay for the tickets."

They were all at the airport when she arrived. All of her brothers and her sister. "This is one of the things we do best," she thought, "this rallying. When family hurts . . . family comes. The gathering of the clan!"

And then it was time to reunite with her mother. As always, she was holding down the fort, with food waiting. A woman of strength and love, moving all of them toward the moment to gather to mourn. For the family was ready to come.

And come they did! Irish families know how to mourn . . . and this family knew well, having buried

Larry—a child and a brother—and now Dad, the first to join their brother in death.

"The general," as he was sometimes affectionately called by his kin, was always the one to don a well-worn suit and tie to attend every wake and funeral that happened in the hundreds of families he knew. And part of his routine was a visit to the cemetery with his home-grown flowers.

So those who loved him now came . . . to love him into his new life and to remember his loving them!

With the old family home long gone, all the family members stayed in the small-town motel. And they filled its rooms with the joy of being together and the pain of the reason! They missed his laughter and his jokes and his wonderful stories. And his children's children missed their "Grandpa Joe." For children were his first love.

Then suddenly the time for the wake had come, and she didn't think she could do it. None of them did. "He looks so thin and little," she thought. "I don't want to remember him this way. I want to remember him big and strong and tan and filled with laughter and stories! I want to remember him loving me!"

But he was so lean and small in the casket. Soon others who loved this giving man began to arrive and to tell the stories of his life. As his friends recalled his antics in grade school and high school and forever in his life, she listened.

The grandkids began to relax, and his presence in the room was felt in those who remembered and loved him. They found him in the stories they told of his loving them.

And then the evening's ritual was complete, and it was the morning of the second day. The time had come to go to where his earthly shell lay in death's slumber. And go they did. Because this was Dad. And Dad would do it for each of them. He would come to say "I love you."

Six days before the Passover, Jesus went to Bethany,
the home of Lazarus, the man he had raised from death.
They prepared a dinner for him there, which Martha
helped serve; Lazarus was one of those who were sitting
at the table with Jesus. Then Mary took a whole pint of
a very expensive perfume made of pure nard, poured it
on Jesus' feet, and wiped them with her hair. The
sweet smell of the perfume filled the whole house.
One of Jesus' disciples, Judas Iscariot—the one who
was going to betray him—said, "Why wasn't this
perfume sold for three hundred silver coins and the
money given to the poor?"

John 12:1–5

*Jesus is with them as they
laugh and as they cry.*

Let's put ourselves there.
We can smell the sweet
scent of oil in that home.
We can hear laughter.
We can touch joy.

Friends are gathered,
perhaps a prearranged dinner party to celebrate the fact
that Lazarus is back with them, raised from the dead by
his good friend Jesus. And of course, Jesus is there. He
has gathered with the two sisters—Martha and Mary—
and their brother, Lazarus.

The wine is flowing; they're probably joking and
laughing and remembering good times spent together.
The food smells great and tastes even better! And then
Mary uncaps the oil to rub on Jesus' feet. And the home
is filled with its wonderful aroma.

Holy are these moments of family with Jesus in the
midst, celebrating new life. And holy are the moments
of the family in our opening story. They have gathered

together to say good-bye to their much loved husband, dad, grandpa, and friend. Jesus is in the midst of them as they mourn, as they eat and drink, as they tell the stories. (The hundreds of stories!)

Jesus is with them as they laugh and as they cry. He is in the children as they wonder if Grandpa is really dead and as they puzzle over why he looks so little in the big box with a lid. Jesus is with this family as friends come and go and pay their respects to this man who in some way touched their lives.

And Jesus is there in the new life they believe in. Jesus is with them forever, living in the person of Joe as he lives on in their memories. Jesus is with them as they remember his tanned face, his hearty laugh, his curly hair, his handsome Irish face, his love of food, his tendency to exaggerate. Jesus is with them because Joe and the way he touched their lives is part of each of them. They are the family Joe loved and his love, now part of the new life of Jesus, is with them through time and into eternity.

Jesus lives in family.

> *This "family of God" is gradually formed and takes shape during the stages of human history, in keeping with the Father's plan.*
>
> CCC, 759

Where God is, good is.

This chapter, which is central to families and to the larger Church, is like the heart of a movie or the crescendo of a symphony or even the tie-breaking goal in a sudden-death overtime game. In this chapter, our beliefs really come home. We discover that our spiritual beliefs are the stuff of ordinary family life, for the life of the family is the most fundamental expression of the love of God in the Church.

The experience of God in the family, whether named or not, enters each person at a fundamentally deep and lasting level. This cannot be denied. God is present as long as genuine love is present and acted on. Already present! We don't need to import God into the family. God is already there.

During the first few years of our life, we are very open, very receptive to what happens to us. However, we are too small to be aware of this. So other people—the adults who are part of our lives—have to know. Those who somehow touch our lives are charged with an awesome responsibility. They hold in their hands our very life and future; they hold in their hands our expectations and dreams.

Obviously, they also hold our expectation of God. Because to us, in those first few years, the grown-ups are "god." Our interaction with others—parents, brothers, sisters, stepparents, stepsiblings, child-care persons, grandparents, teachers, next-door neighbors—influence us forever. For good or not.

In the first chapter of this book, we talked about our hunger to know our God. This hunger is part of what makes us human. Although the hunger in an infant is largely for food, it is also for nourishing human contact.

Through this human contact, the infant comes to trust others—or not to trust them; to trust God—or not to trust God.

Of course, the infant doesn't know that. But we grown-ups do. The mom offers her breast or a bottle to the hungry baby. How she does this feeds the baby's fundamental hunger for love. Knowing that food is there, that when need is felt, someone will care and respond, contributes to the baby's trust in human beings and in God. (We can trust in God's love only if we have been able to trust the "big" people in our lives, only if they have shown themselves trustworthy in their love for us.)

Today, most families are convinced that the family needs fixing. In fact, most of the public discussion of early childhood on talk shows, in popular self-help books, and so on deals more with problems or pathology than with success and health. The result is that our self-esteem as families, as members of families, even as a society has gone further and further down. The more we point fingers, down-grade, put down, blame, and label families, the worse we all feel in our families and in the professions and institutions that work with families.

Enough already! The time has come to honor and affirm the wonderful strengths in families! Rarely do we focus on the reality that God lives in families. But in every family where love abides, we can see and feel and praise very real good that is already there.

Jesus said, "Wherever two or more are gathered . . . I am there with them." If love is present, if the family is struggling to feed its members, if they tuck one another in bed each night, if glasses of water are found in the middle of the night, if laughter is heard and kisses and hugs are felt, if birthday presents are hidden away, and forgiveness felt, and even if a dollar or two is found for an important teen's night out with friends, then there is holiness in this family.

The larger Church (the parish, the diocese, the Vatican, and so on) must proclaim ever more loudly the reality that every family has strengths! Why is this necessary? Because families are like individuals. When we scold and put down a child repeatedly, the child comes to believe that he or she is worthless and then acts that way.

However, the opposite is also true. When we praise and affirm a child, she or he acts on those strengths. Love begets love. Plain and simple. And love is happening in families. In various degrees and ways. And much like a spark in a campfire or fireplace, we need to gently blow or fan that spark for the fire to become greater. Families know this.

As the larger Church becomes more attuned to the reality of the spirituality that is already in families, we will begin to see the family as the first and foremost setting where each of us is formed and encounters the love of the living God! If good is in the family, God is there. If God is there, good is there. This may sound too simple, but the fact is—where God is, good is.

Family as church

In the last chapter, we briefly reflected on the four marks of the Church: one, holy, catholic, and apostolic. Now we will connect these indicators

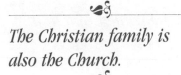

The Christian family is also the Church.

of the larger Church with the four basic tasks (marks) of the Christian family. (1) The Christian family is a community of persons; (2) the Christian family serves life; (3) the Christian family enhances the life of the Church; and (4) the Christian family improves society.

Pope John Paul II, in his crucial writing about the family called *On the Family* ("Familiaris Consortio"), identified these four tasks (marks) of the family.

(This pope is particularly sensitive to the importance of family because of his own personal family history. His mother died when he was a preteen, and then his dad and only sibling, an older brother, died about ten years later when the pope was in his early twenties. Some of the most moving teachings of Pope John Paul II deal with family life.)

Pope John Paul II calls the family "the domestic church." This description of the family is both positive and supportive. It challenges us. The Christian family is not just like the Church, nor are we a miniature version of the Church. *The Christian family is also the church.* But we are not a church identical to the parish or diocesan church, which is a gathering of many households of faith. No. We are a church in our own way, in our own household.

Let us explore then, the tasks/marks of the Church of the home—the domestic church—and see how they coincide with the marks of the larger Church.

Task 1: The family as a community of persons

Each member of a family has a dignity that is rightly hers or his.

The first role or task of the family is to form a community of persons. That is, the family must affirm each and every family member. When we affirm, we help each family member find and use his or her gifts; we nurture each family member; we gently and consistently challenge each family member to grow in loving others. This effective loving of each family member establishes unity in the family. Doing this is a very demanding, often difficult job. But it is deeply, deeply important.

Each member of a family has a dignity that is rightly hers or his. In the larger society, we violate a person's dignity when we treat that person simply as a member of a class of people (for example, as an Asian, a Native American, a New York taxi cab diver, a bishop, a teenager, a lesbian). But we can do this in family too. We can look upon our child simply as a nay-saying two-year-old or as a rebellious teenager. We can see our parents simply as old people. We must resist pigeon-holing one another.

Affirming the full right of all persons to be unique and special is especially important today. The way some adult men treat women is certainly not Christian. (Even some women treat other women in an unChristian way.)

Sometimes the dehumanization of women or men can take on rather subtle forms: One spouse becomes "the parent"; the other "the child"; power is held by one within the home—one leads; the other submits. Or parents may treat their children as mere extensions of themselves, encouraging (manipulating) their children into activities more attuned to the parents' interests. In all these cases, someone is being hurt, controlled, held down, and held back from becoming fully human and fully alive.

The way each family affirms the dignity of its members will vary from family to family. In one family the identification of a family member as "the weird one" could be a genuine term of endearment. Whereas in another family, this phrase would be a first-class put-down. What's important here are the simple, but not insignificant, ways families notice each other, care for each other, struggle with each other, respect each other, and include each other. Simple, basic stuff—but very, very holy.

One of the best indicators of family as a community of persons is the presence of good, honest, and open communication between all the family members. This does not mean that each member always agrees with the others. But it does mean they are talking about their differences, respecting each other in those differences, and working toward agreement.

What we are describing here is a delicate balance between the value of personal autonomy (healthy individuality) and, at the same time, the value of being family—the connectedness. Both are family values. And although a healthy tension exists between them, they are not opposites to each other. If too much autonomy is pushed or sought, the family can break apart. If too much family connectedness is pushed or sought, the unique God-given individual gift of each person may be lost. There needs to be a holy, healthy balance.

Noticing and valuing the special and unique features of each family member are indicators of oneness. (Oneness is the first mark of the larger Church.) However, we do not achieve oneness by uniformity of appearance or behavior. In fact, the totally look-alike, act-alike, think-alike family can be a family without love. It can be a very controlling family that insists on conformity much more than respect for individual differences. Just as in the larger Church, conformity in a family can cause great problems. In other words, it may not be a community of unique persons.

We are family members, each and every one of us. Each of us is created in the image and likeness of God; each of us is a child of God.

Task 2: The family serves life

Holy are those who give drink to the thirsty at three o'clock in the morning.

The second role or task of the family—serving life—coincides with the mark of the larger Church, which is to be holy. As the primary community of persons supporting the dignity of each of its members, the family also is called to be life-giving. This includes bringing children into the world as well as supporting life in all its forms and stages.

The family is holy by being life-giving in a thousand and one ways as it nourishes and supports the life of its members. Caring for life is caring for what's precious to God. Holy are those who give drink to the thirsty at three o'clock in the morning. Holy are those who listen, just listen, to the pain of a teenager learning to love. Holy are those who make hamburger stretch. And holy are those who value each moment of life, in all its messiness or joy.

In valuing its own life, family reaches out to the wider community. The most obvious way of doing this is by supporting life and life-giving decisions. Abortion is most often named here. But we can also deny the value of life by ignoring the forces in society that bring women to the point that abortion seems their only option. When men use and abuse and abandon women and children, they often force them into poverty. All of these actions are antilife. We also denigrate life's value by treating the elderly callously, by ignoring the needs of people who are disabled, or by expressing and acting on our racism and sexism.

A human being need not "qualify" in order to earn the right to life and its necessities. The right to be born and to live a life of dignity, equality, and just treatment comes directly from God.

Pope John Paul II likes to refer to the family as "the first school of love and life." Out of great and abiding love, God creates life. But the family is the co-creator of life. Both God and families create life by loving. Through the love of the couple for each other or the love of a parent for a child or the love of brothers or sisters for one another or the love of a grandparent for a grown child or a grandchild, new life comes forth. Love creates life—life in new human beings and life in relationships. And where love is, there is God.

But loving and creating are not enough; we also have to care for that which we create. That is why the Church describes education as part of the role of family. And, interestingly, the Church here is not referring to college education or law school. No. The Church means the kind of education done in families.

Families are the first school of love and life. The school of the family gives us the knowledge of how to love and be loved, of how to value life in everyone. None of us can succeed as human beings if the school of our family does not teach us how to love. This is our basic education; it is also our most important education!

Task 3: The family church enhances the life of the larger Church

When family is church, it is church in a family way.

The third mark of the larger Church is being catholic (being universally connected to others). The family is catholic when it shares in the life and mission of the larger Church.

To describe the fact that we in family are the church, we use the following terms: the church of the home, the domestic church, the household of faith. As family members, the gentle wind of the Spirit blows between us. This Spirit is God's life made real in the lives of ordinary people.

The Spirit is in us and with us when we try to love one another, in spite of the difficulties of doing so! The Spirit dwells with us and in us when we die to self for others and when we welcome new life. The Spirit lives in us and with us when we reconnect after hurt or misunderstanding. After reconciliation, the family does not return to where it was before forgiveness. Instead, the family creates a new way of being together.

When family is church, it is church in a family way. For example, parents don't address their children like a priest offering a homily (sermon) at Mass, but rather in ordinary conversational language. In ordinary holy language of the home, they communicate aspects of God's love and concern for the family, and all others. Thus, the family is the church, happening right now.

Task 4: The family serves society

The fourth mark of the larger Church is that of being apostolic. That is, the Church brings the message of Jesus to the outside world. Likewise, the family

Family and society are responsible to and for each other.

has a responsibility to other families in the neighborhood, the town, the city, and beyond. While one's own family brings lots of challenges and lots of important moments, it ought not to be the whole story of one's life. Families have doors and windows and the television. The outside world is seen and connects with the family in many key ways.

Family members have a relationship with and an obligation to life in the wider society. The family's spirit of love and caring is extended into other families because our yards connect and our children play together; because we stand together in the check-out line at the grocery store and we sit in the doctor's office and worry together; because we sing together at Mass or work together in the office. We are a part of one another's lives. Families affect and are affected by other families. The Church invites us to interact with other families with the same love and concern we give to our own family.

As we know, within the family we learn the patterns of behavior most needed by society. For example, in our family we first learn how to show respect for others; how to share, cooperate, and work together; how to express our concern for the poor; how to seek justice.

Family and society are responsible to and for each other. The basic community of family is forever linked to and a part of the wider community. The wider community is likewise a part of every family. One needs and is needed by the other. There is a partnership. Thus, family values are also society's values and vice versa!

Society (other families and the institutions that serve the family) has a responsibility to provide the opportunity for a family to be family. Personal rights exist and so do family rights. Thus, we need to establish those economic and social conditions that help the family survive and thrive. The health of both society and family depends on this.

A society that deprives the family of the opportunity to earn an adequate living is a society in deep trouble. We see this society in trouble when it creates laws and systems that discourage and deprive the family of an opportunity to be together; when its employment, education, or health-care structures support themselves, rather than the family. (For example, most employers readily listen to a worker explain that he or she is late because the car broke down; many employers are less willing to listen to an explanation about a sick child.) We must place the family first in our society. By not doing so, we break society apart because we break apart its most basic component—the family.

So strong, healthy families build strong, healthy societies. The two go together. The same holds true for the various structures of the Church. If the family is alive, hopeful, and loving, this will spread to the rest of the Church. We are all connected. And we are all one family under God.

> *Family is about God being between and among us.*

We label adults in our culture as married or not. For example, saying "he is single" means he is not married. Widowed means a spouse died. Divorced or separated means some stage of being out of the married state. And a "married couple" is the criterion from which these other conditions are named.

Is there anything wrong with this? Some single persons might say so, especially if they are single because they are priests or vowed religious (sisters or brothers). Other single people might object for other reasons. But what naming a person single really tells us is that a person is not in a family as a result of marriage. This illustrates how central the family state is in our culture. We name a person's state in life in relation to family.

Is this to say that single people are not family? Of course not! To be born into the human family is what makes one a member of a family. And therefore, all of us qualify!

Of course, some people also then go on to create a new family through marriage. A childless couple still qualifies as a family. A single parent and her or his child are also a family. Two siblings living together qualify as a family. A divorced person with grown children still qualifies as a family. And so forth.

Being family includes those who are married and not married. Family membership is an inclusive reality because our God is an inclusive God. To say otherwise is tantamount to denying the sacredness of humanity. In fact, it is even to classify Jesus as not being family!

Family is about relationships; it's about God being between and among the members; it's about loving and being in a household of faith.

We can never undo being family. God is there.

A Psalm

The Lord is king,
 and he rules the nations.
All proud people will bow down to him;
 all mortals will bow down before him.
Future generations will serve him;
 they will speak of the Lord to the coming generation.
People not yet born will be told:
 "The Lord saved his people."

Psalm 22:28–31

Holy Family

e, in family, know, dear God,
That whenever we act
from that precious place called love,
It is holy.

Help us, then,
To help those who don't understand
That holiness is present
In the millions of
Big and little ways we love one another.

That it doesn't mean we have to go
Anywhere.

That our home
Is already a holy place too,
Like other holy places.
Already holy, O God. Already holy.

And you know, and we know,
Dear God,
That we don't always have to do anything else
 either.
Just continue . . .
Remembering you . . .
In the way we love one another.
Amen.

CHAPTER TWELVE

Our Hope for Eternal Happiness

That old connection was there.

Jim saw his colleague coming down the hall toward him and greeted him with the usual cheery smile and hello. But his friend remained somber. Something was wrong.

"Paul, what's the matter?" he asked with concern.

"Don died this morning."

He couldn't believe what he'd just heard. "What?" he exclaimed.

His friend Don had been thirty-eight. Yesterday . . . yesterday, they'd been together! Their two families were very close. And today he was dead! It was almost beyond belief. "Don! Dead! Oh, my God," he tried to absorb the reality.

The rituals of death somehow came and went. Jim and his family helped his friend's widow and the kids as much as possible. But it was so hard; the two families had been so close, and Don was gone. Eventually, his bereaved family moved away. The two families tried to stay connected. They even saw each other from time to time, but everything was so different.

Years passed. Then one summer, when the widow was home visiting Don's family, the two families got together. Much had happened in both families' journeys. But that old connection was there; it always would be.

Don was buried in this "home" city, so Jim asked Don's widow if she and the kids visited the cemetery when they came. Her answer was quick, simple, and profound. And he never forgot it.

"He's not there," she said.

"Heaven is the ultimate end and fulfillment of the deepest human longings, the state of supreme, definitive happiness."

CCC, 1024

"Then the King will say to the people on his right,
'Come, you that are blessed by my Father! Come and
possess the kingdom which has been prepared for you
ever since the creation of the world. I was hungry and
you fed me, thirsty and you gave me drink; I was a
stranger and you received me in your homes, naked and
you clothed me; I was sick and you took care of me,
in prison and you visited me.' The righteous will then
answer him, 'When, Lord, did we ever see you hungry
and feed you, or thirsty and give you a drink? When did
we ever see you a stranger and welcome you in our
homes, or naked and clothe you? When did we ever see
you sick or in prison, and visit you?' The King will reply,
'I tell you, whenever you did this for one of the least
important of these followers of mine, you did it for me!' "

Matthew 25:34–40

*Out of goodness and
kindness comes
reward.*

This scriptural passage
makes all of us squirm.
Sometimes we don't want
to listen to this one
because it hits too close
to home. But today, let's
read it from a positive
perspective. Let's choose to love in practical, down-to-
earth ways. Our God is as close as our neighbor. And
who is our neighbor? Let's look around. Our neighbor
is everywhere, everyone.

The passage from Matthew's gospel provides us
with a map that points out special love opportunities.
We can help others who have basic unmet needs. (We
cannot get more basic than food, clothing, and shelter.)
But note, too, that the passage does not describe organized charity. The subject of each sentence is "you."

When *you* fed the hungry, *you* gave drink to the thirsty, *you* clothed, *you* cared, and *you* visited. You . . . not someone in your name with your money.

The implications for the family are obvious. No other community deals with providing the basics more than the family does. And the family does this at all times and in all stages of life—from when we are born into one until we die.

And the demands of responding to all these basic needs of others (and don't forget our own needs) can be quite demanding. Acts of generosity in the family rarely bring forth applause. Nor do they get into the newspaper. But that does not decrease their importance—for the person helped, for the helper, and for God!

We easily forget the thousands or millions of times we did exactly what the Gospel says. Yes, *we* forget, but God always remembers. God has an exceedingly good memory.

In our opening story of the husband who died in his early years, his widow knew, perhaps more than anyone else, of his kindness and love. And because of this, she knew where he was. Not under the ground, but with the God who dreamed him into life; witnessed his goodness; and brought him to eternal life, filled with the goodness and the love of God.

We cannot give without receiving—sometimes here, sometimes later, but always we will receive that which was prepared for us since the foundation of the world.

"God is preparing a new dwelling . . ."

CCC, 1048

We will live forever.

In the beginning, God created life. In the end, God sustains life. From our Christian perspective, we will never, ever die to God. God invites us to share God's life forever. This truth of our faith is almost too good to be true.

The Apostles' Creed ends with: I believe in . . . the communion of saints, the forgiveness of sins, the resurrection of the body, and the life everlasting.

What do we believe? Each of us believes in the communion of saints. God calls us to be saints, that is, to love one another. And all who respond to God's invitation are already or will be with God forever. We dream of being in the communion of saints, playing and laughing with them and with God.

Second, we believe in the forgiveness of sins. We believe that our loving God forgives all our failings out of God's unbounded generosity, out of God's unconditional love for us. The God who is love, the Being of Love, will have the final word.

Third, we believe in the resurrection of the body. This body is not just a part of us; it is us. The apostle Thomas placed his hands in the wounds of Jesus after the resurrection. What does that mean? It means that Jesus' risen body still had identifying marks.

Will this be true for us? We want to believe that who we are now and what we will experience later will somehow be connected. We don't know for sure, but we need to think about these things and to believe that they will happen in some way.

Fourth, we believe in the life everlasting. We will live forever. Imaging this is hard. In truth, we can't imagine life everlasting. No one can. Even when people seem to know what this is all about, they don't. They just know what others know. But that's okay.

We believe that we are on the way to something wonderful. We live in the hope that life everlasting will happen for us—and for all those we are close to. God wishes exactly the same thing.

Beyond our best dreams

Abiding beauty and love. Jesus did not intend Christians to be abstract, glum, or sad. We sometimes forget this. Even Church leaders forget this and take on a sour look. Years ago, the Catholic Church often sponsored what were called missions that were given in the parish church.

The mission was like the Catholic version of the revival meeting. Sometimes these missions presented the faith like a scary movie. Lots of fire and brimstone, hell fire and damnation, doom and gloom. But fear is a terrible condition on which to build a vibrant Christian faith. Our God is a God of love, celebration, laughter, closeness, warmth, and joy. Our God is not a God of fear.

In the past, the Church often described heaven as a place where we would be given the beatific vision, which means directly seeing God in all God's beauty. This contrasts to the way we experience God now, which is never direct. In heaven, we will see God as God is.

What is the reality of God? Who is God? Well, if we take all that is beautiful and good in creation—people, animals, nature, the galaxies, the pictures of the earth from space—and then add all that we have not yet seen in the universe (which is immense), we would still not have touched the surface of the answer to our question. All of this is but a pale, pale shadow of the abiding beauty and goodness and love of our God.

God invites us to live life fully, to be fully alive. That is God's permanent hope for us. That is why we were created. So, we can assume that the life ahead—life everlasting—will be far more than the very best moments of our life here! Heaven will be loving and being loved for all eternity; knowing and being known. We will be caught up in God. And God is love.

The now connects with the eternal future

The kingdom of God is at hand. It's here. It's around us. It's between us. In the beginning of Mark's gospel

Every act of love is forever.

we are clued in to what's happening, and it's the "Big Time"—the time of expectation. The kingdom has started. Its fulfillment is not complete; we haven't seen the whole play, but the curtain's gone up. The show has started.

And now we are somewhere between the start and the finish. Perhaps right in the middle. The kingdom began with Jesus and will extend beyond the end of the earth, because the kingdom of God is forever.

Now we come to the punch line. Every time we act with simple kindness, every time we forgive, every time we reach out in life-giving love, the kingdom grows. In and through and with Jesus Christ, the kingdom of God takes roots, stretches out its branches, reaches upward and outward and inward; the kingdom of God grows. And the kingdom will continue to grow in time and through eternity. Each and every act of love is forever.

These days our society emphasizes the "right now." Of course, what happens in the present *is* important. We can think that the past is what was and the future is what will be and what is happening now is the present. And we seem to have only the now.

But what went before and what we imagine is coming makes up the now of our life. So all aspects of time are important. Today, however, our society focuses more on the present than on the past or the future. There is a certain sadness to this because the future is powerfully important. Our idea of the future is what draws us ahead. Expectation is part of the fun.

Another factor influencing the eclipse of future concerns is that we live in a youth-oriented culture. To the young, growing old is neither exciting nor is it something to look forward to. Many young people live not so much as if there is no tomorrow, but as if they don't want a tomorrow!

These trends serve to put a wall between us and our future. And we don't want any doors in that wall. We want to stay young. Like Peter Pan, we don't want to grow up. And most of all, we don't want to die. We fear that once we die, it's all over. It's *all* over.

Our faith reminds us that we were created by the eternal God. God wants to give us happiness for all eternity.

In our Catholic tradition, we tell of a figure who stands at the gates of heaven. His name is Peter, and we read in the sixteenth chapter of Matthew's gospel that before Jesus ascended into heaven, he gave Peter "the keys to the kingdom." Part of his reason for selecting Peter might be that Peter had rejected Jesus. Thus, this simple fisherman knew what being forgiven meant. He knew about rejection and forgiveness not as a theory, but from personal experience.

The passage about Peter and his power over the "gates" is filled with a sense of forgiveness and welcoming, not fear and rejection. In other words, the keys are given to open the gates and not to keep them locked! Peter's job is to let people in!

This is the spirit of the gospels. This is God's fundamental attitude toward us as revealed by Jesus. We are loved into life. We are loved during life. We are loved at the end of our life here, and we are loved in welcome through the gates beyond. We are Easter people, hopeful people, and happy people living ordinary holiness, because that's the way God wants life to be. Forever and ever. Amen.

Load up on random acts of spontaneous kindness.

We've all heard the saying "You can't take it with you!" This quip refers to the taking of earthly possessions to the next life. For example, we can't take our Chevy Cavalier, our basset hound, our IRA, or our favorite fishing rod. All this stays behind. The old saying can cut deep. If we can't take these things with us, then we had better not live as if we could. We'd best not spend a lot of time and energy on them, for they are perishable goods.

Is there anything that we can take with us? Yes!

We can keep "matters of the heart." That's similar to an image used by Jesus himself. Where our heart is, there is our treasure. And treasures of this kind are allowed to "go with us."

In the medieval morality play called *Everyman* (renamed *Everyperson* in a contemporary version), various actions converse with the main character, our friend Everyperson, about what's really important in life. One of the characters in the play is called "Good Deeds." In the Christian perspective we are using here, good deeds will stay with us forever.

So here are some tips for the big journey. Load up on good deeds, especially random acts of spontaneous kindness. Store wholesome memories, for they are allowed through the gate. The more envy, impatience, small-mindedness, mean-spiritedness, anger you can get rid of, the easier you will travel.

Nothing of goodness will be lost. Some of us are given a very short time. Some a lot. Why? We don't know. Nevertheless, time is given to us each day as an opportunity to fill in with good thoughts, good words, and good actions. Life-giving thoughts, words, and actions. Life pressed down and overflowing—now and throughout eternity.

A Psalm

The Lord is loving and merciful, / slow to become
angry and full of constant love. / He is good to
everyone / and has compassion on all he made. /
All your creatures, Lord, will praise you, / and all your
people will give you thanks. / They will speak of the
glory of your royal power / and tell of your might, /
so that everyone will know your mighty deeds / and
the glorious majesty of your kingdom. / Your rule is
eternal, / and you are king forever.

Psalm 145:8–13

This Family's Gettin' Ready, Lord

Here we are, Lord Jesus,
We're working hard!
And some of us are even
more ready, Lord,
Cuz' we've been here longer.
But all of us are workin'
In whatever way we do,
In school,
At home,
In the yard.
Even when we are a havin' fun, Lord,
We're gettin' ready.
And although we don't
Really understand "forever"
Because nothin' we know, Lord Jesus,
Ever lasts that long,
We are still a-hopin'
An' we are still a-prayin'
That your promise is true.
'Cuz you see, Lord,
Our family . . .
We believe. Amen.